Spirituality
Recharted

Hubert van Zeller

ST. BEDE'S PUBLICATIONS
Petersham, Massachusetts

Published by St. Bede's Publications
Box 545
Petersham, Massachusetts 01366

9 8 7 6 5 4 3 2

Nihil Obstat   Lawrence A. Deery, J.C.L.
Vicar for Canonical Affairs
Judicial Vicar, Diocese of Worcester

Imprimatur   +Timothy J. Harrington
Bishop of Worcester

July 17, 1985

The *Nihil Obstat* and *Imprimatur* are official declarations that a book is considered to be free of doctrinal and moral error. It is not implied that those who have granted the *Nihil Obstat* and *Imprimatur* necessarily agree with the contents, opinions or statements expressed.

LIBRARY OF CONGRESS CATALOGING IN PUBLICATION DATA

Van Zeller, Hubert, 1905-1984
  Spirituality recharted.

  Includes bibliographical references.
  1. Spirituality—Catholic Church.   2. Catholic Church—Doctrines.
I. Title.
BX2350.2.V1935   1985   248.2'2   85-8252
ISBN 0-932506-39-9

To the memory of M.D.K.
who told us juniors fifty years ago
what books to read

CONTENTS

PREFACE

In case the title should give the impression that the author has something new to bring forward which puts the accepted authorities in a back place, this is far from the intention of the book. Rather the reverse. The word "recharted" is meant to suggest, and encourage, a going over of the old ground. The reader is urged to consult such classical writers as Dionysius, St. John of the Cross, St. Teresa of Avila, Tauler, Walter Hilton, the author of *The Cloud of Unknowing,* and others in the same tradition who have mapped the spiritual journey but whose directions have, in our less patient age, been neglected. To change the metaphor from cartography to painting in oils, an artist has to be careful in the early stages of his picture not to get too far away from the charcoal drawing; paint has a way of taking over the original design. In the same way a soul of prayer must be careful not to overlay the original patterns of spirituality with rituals and devotions. This is not to say that the traditional ways of the spirit, as formulated by the well-known teachers, are meant to be followed so rigidly as to stifle personal inclination (anymore than the painter's brush must be kept to the rough sketch), but there has to be some sort of order and discipline about spirituality (and about painting) or the whole undertaking becomes amorphus and empirical.

Now that there is a marked revival of interest in the life of the spirit it seems a good time to do some revision. Not necessarily to review the "set books" one by one, as though insisting on a course of required reading, but more as looking in general to the tried doctrine of the experts. The advanced no less than the beginners need to know that what they have set themselves to work at is safe from false mysticism, is the way of truth. But there is more to it than merely playing safe and going by the guidelines. Occasions arise, and must arise, when grace either obscures the guidelines, so that the soul cannot see what to do next, or else calls to a way of faith for which rules and precedents are no help. Not that the guidelines are to be arbitrarily jumped but that they are not understood. Sanctity, spirituality, self-giving—these things mean more than keeping the rules. When a young man once asked Noel Coward how to become a good actor he got the answer his question deserved: "Just speak your lines distinctly, dear, and don't bump into the furniture." Sanctity is more than repeating the script and not bumping into sin. It is the pursuit of sanctity by responding to the grace of spirituality that this book hopes to promote.

People talk of a "school" of spirituality, as of a school of art or literature, reflecting a particular time, country, trend, or spirit. Thus you get Franciscan and Jesuit schools, Spanish and Flemish, Christian and Zen. You might as well talk of a school of happiness, a school of marriage, a school of suffering. Spirituality is spirituality whichever way you look at it. Discussion of, and comparisons between, Western and Eastern spirituality may be fuel for the card-index but is not necessarily fuel for prayer. Anyway the method of approach to be found in the present work will be to follow roughly St. John of the Cross' treatment of the soul's progress towards union with God. Whatever the contributing factors towards the practice of contemplative prayer, St. John's exposition can be taken as describing the most common experience of interior souls. Granted that no two souls are alike and that the Holy Spirit acts in whatever way he wills, there yet remains a definitive way of responding to Christ who is himself the way. By responding to the way, the soul comes to see deeper into the truth and participates more fully in the life. Any account of the spiritual journey must stress this primary quality of response (which differs both from the acknowledgment of God's omnipresence which is given in faith and from the application of acknowledgment to daily life which is expressed in moral conduct), and so seek to direct all the soul's energies towards developing this response.

Finally I must thank the editors of St. Bede's Publications for kindly allowing me to use material from an article I wrote for the 1981 issue of *Word and Spirit,* and for their patience in checking and correcting the references in that article which have been used again in this book.

SPIRITUALITY RECHARTED

CHAPTER 1
Preparation

GOD DOES NOT FORCE SPIRITUALITY on us. He offers it and lets us take it or leave it. Assuming we accept the grace, God builds up on our acceptance and eventually, with our cooperation, we come to live more and more in the spirit and become contemplatives. But there has to be a deliberate turning to him at the outset, a purposeful conversion.[1] Though dramatic and miraculous conversions do take place, they are infrequent in the history of spirituality. The classic example of St. Paul's conversion on the road to Damascus, unique as it is, may nevertheless be taken as symbolic of the soul's first experience of the spiritual life: the summons, the bewilderment, the sense of being led in a particular direction, the ability to see with a new vision. The full revelation of God's plan did not come all at once to St. Paul and it does not come all at once to us. He had first to turn away from his old life before he could put on the new. He had to learn, accept guidance from others, form a completely different understanding of life, and give himself to the service of prayer. All this took time, and only when he had mastered new ways of thinking and acting was he made ready to do what the Holy Spirit had all along been planning for him. Paul's missionary journeys, and after these his letters from prison, were his life's work and for this he needed the training and practice of prayer. He needed to search for God dwelling within himself. By the time he

---

[1]Père Garrigou-Lagrange, in *The Three Ways of the Spiritual Life,* writes of three conversions: the first (p. 16) from a life of sin; the second (ch. 2) when the soul enters into the Illuminative Way; the third (ch. 3) when the soul enters the Unitive Way. The author explains at some length the way in which the twelve apostles passed from one conversion to another.

was preaching in Athens he gives a hint of his spiritual odyssey when he says that men should "seek God, grope after him and find him" (Acts 17:27). It is eveybody's spiritual odyssey.

Allowing for diversities of calls and diversities of spirits, suppose a soul becomes aware of God's increasing attraction within. What next? What has to be done to follow up this attraction? Prayer for further light is obviously the first thing. No preparation for the interior life can even get started without that. Preparation differs from initiation —preparation denotes activity on the soul's part, initiation denotes activity on God's. Reading prepares the mind and heart; direction from someone who knows what he is talking about helps; retreats and days set aside for ruminating help; but prayer is the chief factor in creating the disposition to go ahead with the spiritual life. "Prepare your hands to stretch out to him" (Job 11:13). "Prepare yourself for the search" (Job 8:8). "Turn to the Lord with all your heart, put away strange gods, prepare your hearts to the Lord and serve him only" (1 Sam. 7:3). This last quotation gives it all: conversion from, conversion to, the decision to give total service. Until the strange gods of materialism: worldly ways of thinking, devaluation of divine law and Scripture, cheating in loyalty to the Church—until all that is opposed to the life of grace has been put away, the soul cannot expect to find true spirituality.

It is unfashionable today to praise, or even quote from, *The Imitation of Christ,* but it is nevertheless the book which has been most translated and published after the Bible, and has helped souls for centuries. It is accused of being Jansenistic in tone, negative, depressing. Admittedly it does not jolly the reader along with joyful tidings, welcoming the newly converted to the contemplative club, but then neither does St. John of the Cross. The point is it prepares the soul for what lies ahead, it tells of the trials the soul is in for. St. Teresa has a lighter touch, so has Sister Elizabeth of the Trinity, but all great mystical writers teach the same doctrine that you will find in the pages of the *Imitation:* "Son, when thou comest to the service of God, make thyself ready to endure tribulation." How could the total service of God, the complete surrender which echos the preaching of Christ from the cross, be otherwise? "I thirst," our Lord said, and the thirst was not only of his tongue and throat. It was from his Sacred Heart which thirsted for souls who would volunteer to join him in his most characteristic act of suffering and dying for love.

If it is objected that the hopeful beginner will only be put off by this sort of talk, and that if the cross is presented to him too starkly he will steer clear of spirituality, there is St. Paul's exhortation to the Corinthians to be considered: "Everyone in a contest abstains from all things, and they indeed to obtain a perishable crown but we an imperishable one...I treat my body hard and bring it into subjection" (1 Cor. 9:25-27). There are not many universal laws in life but one of them is that we value what we have worked for more than we value what is handed to us on a plate. Spirituality is not handed to us on a plate, and preparation for it is not a trust-to-luck process.

So we are examining a soul who, at some cost, is "walking in newness of life" (Rom 6:4). It is always stimulating to make a new start, and Scripture is always urging us to do so. "I will put a new spirit in them," said Ezekiel (11:19), and again "Renounce your sins, avoid all occasions of sin...and make yourselves a new heart and a new spirit" (18:31). Psychologically, spiritually, and even commercially the value of newness is recognized. Whether it is an outlook or a toothpaste we are urged to take our stand on something new. "Fights cavities," proclaims the new brand; "faces cavities," proclaims the psychiatrist; "fill up cavities," proclaims the prophet. Into the void of our characters, into the nothingness which we are so careful to hide from ourselves, the grace of God is poured so that we become new beings in Christ. In our rare moments of humility we accuse ourselves of being shallow, but of course we are not shallow at all. We are so deep that only an infinite God can supply our want. Without God the walls of our souls echo to our emptiness, but with God we grow into the beings we were designed to be—we become *alteri Christi,* other Christs.

So the spiritual life is a matter of cooperation, an exchange, a joint movement. Prayer, which is the specific act of spirituality, can be compared to chess. There has to be a certain knowledge of what is required, there are moves and conventions to be learned, what one player does depends upon what the other does, when the opening move is followed by the move from the opposite side of the board the game is in play. The opening move is always the Holy Spirit's. This illustration is woefully inadequate because for one thing the soul is not playing against God but with him, and for another the aim is not to win but to go on playing.[2] Also you play chess with your head whereas you pray with your heart.

So in the reciprocal relationship of prayer the soul is both the loved and the lover, the sought and the seeker. God too is at once the loved and lover, sought and seeker. But the initiative is always with grace. "It is God who puts into you both the will and the performance" (Phil. 2:13). When we think we are doing all, we find it is God who is doing all. The desire to do all for God is the first step towards knowing that we have done nothing. When we think we have acquitted ourselves fairly creditably as regards the text, "Be converted to me with all your heart. . . rend your heart and turn to the Lord your God" (Joel 2:12), we discover to our shame that, though in theory our hearts have been converted, they remain much what they always were when counter-attractions to God's love come along. It is the heart that God wants, not the theory.

A question now comes up to which in spiritual literature contradictory answers have been given. Does God call all souls to this heartfelt conversion and total surrender which is the condition for contemplative prayer or is the summons only to the few? In other words is the grace of contemplation something we must all aspire to or don't we

---

[2]There is the puzzling story in Gen. 32:24-30 which tells of Jacob wrestling with an angel. Still more surprising is that he won. In a footnote to this incident, *The New American Bible*, which is based on the Douay Version of the Old Testament, comments as follows: "The angel was in human shape. . . he is called God (28 and 30) because he represented the person of the Son of God. This wrestling, in which Jacob, assisted by God, was a match for an angel, was so ordered that he might learn by this experiment of the divine assistance that neither Esau nor any other man should have power to hurt him. It was also spiritual, as appears by his earnest prayer, urging, and at last obtaining, the angel's blessing." Anyway the precedent, if such a conflict should ever arise, is not one to be followed. A soul may have to spend all night wrestling with temptation or distraction but this is something quite different—he is not wrestling with grace.

stand a chance if our names are not on the list? The answer is somewhat Delphic, depending upon the interpretation given to what our Lord said on three occasions. Twice he said that "many are called but few are chosen" (Mt. 20:16 and 22:14)[3] and once, speaking of the narrow gate and hard way that leads to life, "few are they that find it" (Mt. 7:14). Admittedly in this latter instance he is referring to eternal life, salvation, but by implication, and logically, the spiritual life is included. These sayings of our Lord have been applied to the Jews who would have a difficult time responding to the call to become Christians, but again they can apply equally to the many souls who are called to contemplation, few of whom ever find it. Taking the texts as they stand, either you say "all are called to contemplative prayer and high perfection, but God sees from the start that some would never be up to it so drops them out," or you say "all *could* make it to the goal to which God is inviting them but only a few take the trouble to make themselves worthy of getting there." We can form a rough idea of how grace works without plunging ourselves into determinism. "Pray for us, O holy Mother of God," we pray, "that we may be made worthy of the promises of Christ." Of ourselves we are not worthy, and never shall be, so we ask Mary's prayers that she may dispose us for what Christ promises. The promises hold good if, by making use of the graces which accompany them, we try to make ourselves worthy of them. We depend not on any merits of ours, but upon the infinite merits of Christ. Until we are convinced of this truth we cannot arrive at the humility which is the condition of all that is to follow.

So you get this: while some would hold that no desire or effort is of any use in meriting the contemplative vocation, others would claim that to those whose hearts and minds are sincerely open to it the grace inevitably follows. Those of each opinion must bear in mind that, like every other grace, the grace of contemplative prayer is a gratuitous gift. "What have you that you have not received?" (1 Cor. 4:7); "the grace in me has not been void" (1 Cor. 15:10). You and I are nothing. Even Paul is nothing. God is all.

St. John of the Cross answers the question as to who is and who is

---

[3] The repetition is taken by some authorities to be due to a mistake on the part of a scribe.

not called to contemplation when he says, "God does not reserve such a lofty vocation to certain souls only; on the contrary he wills that all should embrace it. Yet he finds few who permit him to work such sublime things in them."[4] St. Teresa is not so sure about contemplation being for everybody. "It does not follow," she says, "that because all of us in this house practice prayer we are necessarily contemplatives . . . contemplation is not necessary for salvation, and God does not ask it of us before he gives us our reward."[5] St. John himself seems to have second thoughts when he says, "God does not raise to contemplation everyone who is tried by the Spirit. Not even half of them, and he knows the reason."[6] And again in the same context, "Thus there are many who, when he sends them trials, shrink from the labor and refuse to endure the dryness and mortification. . . hence, finding them to be deficient in strength and cooperation with the first graces he has bestowed upon them he withholds (further graces), and their purification ceases." So it looks as if we are back where we were—two camps: one holding that no desire or effort is of any use in meriting the contemplative vocation, the other claiming that to those whose hearts and minds are open to it the grace inevitably follows. Bearing in mind that the grace of contemplation is a gratuitous gift and cannot strictly be "merited," might not both opinions be satisfied if a distinction is made between all who are *called* and those who are *raised*? In his handling of the contemplative vocation God is not practicing favoritism. All could be favorites if all chose to be. For his part God does not restrict his choice; it is we who are afraid to qualify for it. God shakes out the chessmen from the box and challenges everybody to the game It would be a bad day if nobody wanted to play.

Arising out of the above quotation from St. John of the Cross, which says that God finds some souls who begin well but are not strong enough to meet the hardships along the way so brings their purification to an end, a new difficulty presents itself. In fact it is the age-old

[4]*Living Flame*, 2:5.
[5]*Way of Perfection*, ch. 17 no. 2.
[6]*Living Flame*, no. 2.

od's foreknowledge with man's independ-
most of questions suggest themselves. Can
s in a soul's progress? If he knew that the
graces of contemplation why did he issue
Clearly God could not have misread the
surrender and have discovered too late that
going on with. Let it be said at once that you
to have the mystery of the Blessed Trinity
on between God's providential knowledge
though impossible to clear up, the apparent
n the form of—of all things—a television

hed a long-running series which has taken a
altons or the Ingalls) over a number of years.
ens, the authorities decide to repeat some of
u see the children as you knew them before
dults, you see this week's adults twelve years
younger. Not make-up younger and older but actually younger and
older. Watching again the early sequences, you know more about the
future of the characters than they do themselves. You even know more
than the scriptwriter and director, who will (freely) decide later on
what changes need to be made in the plot, in the location, in the cast.
For them, all this lies ahead; not for you. For you, watching the early
episodes, there is *foreknowledge*. The difference between God's foreknowledge and yours is that he sees the whole series simultaneously.
Where the human mind can trace a continuity, the divine mind sees
succession in unity.

So when the soul who aspires to contemplation aspires no longer, it
doesn't mean that God must change his plan but that the soul has
changed *his* plan. It doesn't mean that God should have given more
grace at the beginning—because God always gives the appropriate
graces for the appropriate works—but that the soul miscalculated its
generosity. The reason why this subject has been given so much space
may not be clear. It is because we are always miscalculating our
generosity. It is one thing to act on a generous impulse and another to
serve God in generosity. Generosity is perseverance in service, espe-

cially in the service of faith. Unless the soul faces this at the start of his journey towards God he is not likely to finish, or even to get far. It is a foolish director who advises the would-be neophyte to "strike out nobly here and now and don't count the cost. . . meet the trials when the time comes but don't think about that yet." This sort of counsel has led to the falling away of souls who have started off with the best intentions and highest hopes. In the strictly spiritual life instances of this are not infrequent, but in the priestly and religious life the reason for failure to persevere until death can nearly always be traced to a lack of understanding at the outset as to what the vocation involved. "Which of you, wishing to build a tower, does not first sit down and calculate the outlays that are necessary whether he has means to complete it? Lest after he has laid the foundation and is not able to finish, all who are looking on begin to mock him saying, 'This man began to build but was unable to finish' " (Lk. 14:28-30).

To build a spiritual tower is a lot harder than to build one of bricks and mortar. Even when the soul has sat down and calculated the outlays that he thinks will be needed, even when he has laid the foundations of penitence and self-surrender, he will still have to budget for losses along the way. The losses will be his fault, not God's. If his self-giving is genuine he will depend upon God's grace to carry him through and not upon any strength of his own. "I can do all things in him who strengthens me" (Phil. 4:13). "Without me you can do nothing" (Jn. 15:5). So in order to make himself ready—not in order to make himself worthy, because nobody can make himself worthy, but in order to make himself ready—the soul must be sure of the genuineness of the resolve. As we shall see on a later page, the soul, in making out the blank check, has no idea of what he is letting himself in for but at least he is counting on God more than on his own generosity. This is the only preparation for the life of prayer which is to follow.

CHAPTER 2
Initiation

HAVING GOTTEN THE SOUL PAST the preliminary stage, called by Garrigou-Lagrange the first conversion, by St. John of the Cross, the active night of the senses, and which is traditionally classified as "the Way of Purgation," we must now consider the stage in which God takes a stronger hand. During St. John's first night the soul is busy renouncing what is seen to be inconsistent with serious conversion (such as deliberate sin, the occasions of sin, inordinate affection, unnecessary luxury and self-indulgence, and, as far as possible, imperfection generally). On the positive side the soul is keeping regular hours of prayer, is trying to practice habitual recollection, is submitting to superiors and to rules. Vocal and mental prayer are accepted readily as part of the discipline, and though not much progress is felt to be made, the effort to master the techniques as prescribed in the textbooks is judged to be infinitely worthwhile, and often, though by no means always, enjoyed. In relation to people there is the earnest purpose to be kind and helpful to everybody. At this stage, however, the inwardness of charity has not been fully understood—charity is seen as acts done for others and not as life lived in Christ. Nor has dependence upon God gone beyond giving a grateful but notional assent to his providential protection. Faith is present of course but only of a rudimentary kind, namely the kind that believes in doctrines, miracles, the value of suffering, and the need to go ahead without doubting the authenticity of the call to interior prayer; but it is not yet the kind that can remain blindly faithful when everything in the intellectual, emotional, spiritual, and even physical life is pulling the other way.

Before we can treat of the new phase upon which the soul is now entering, and which amounts to the first experience of infused contemplation, it would avoid confusion if the terminology of the mystical life were clarified. When St. John of the Cross is talking about the passive night of the "senses" he is referring not to the outward senses of taste, touch, hearing, and so on, but to the interior senses of memory, imagination, and the emotions. These more subtle senses or appetites have to be purified before the soul can enter the region where the intellect and will can be counted upon to exercise the command. The time will come later when intellect and will must also be purified but for the time being, and until the earlier stages of the Illuminative Way have done their work, it is the lower faculties of the soul that call for attention.

Again as regards terminology, the "Illuminative Way" does not denote a way bathed in light, a way in which obscurities are made clear, but rather the opposite. After the first dawn following the night of the senses, when there is indeed a sense of discovery and illumination, the Illuminative Way is for the most part passed in darkness. This darkness is the theme of such works as *The Cloud of Unknowing, The Hid Divinity* of Dionysius the Areopagite, *The Dark Night of the Soul* by St. John of the Cross, and it runs through the writings of Ramon Lull, John Tauler, de Osuna, Arintero, St. Thérèse of Lisieux, Poulain, and Dom John Chapman.[1]

But to go back to the first "dawn," when the action of God begins to replace the action of the soul—the soul's function now is not so much to perfect itself as to allow itself to be perfected by God. The contemplative act is essentially one of receiving rather than one of giving. It supposes surrender, which is giving, but the giving of acceptance is higher in the scale of faith. To sacrifice the tree, as St. Thérèse of Lisieux points out, is greater than to sacrifice its fruits; the fruits are a

[1]St. Teresa of Avila deals with the subject in Chap. 31 of her *Way of Perfection*, but whereas the other authorities mentioned make a treatise out of it, she brings it in almost as an aside. It is the most important chapter in the book. To the names listed in the text might be added those of Hugh and Richard of St. Victor, Ruysbroeck, and Denis the Carthusian, whose treatment is not as precise as can be found in St. John of the Cross and Dionysius.

seasonal offering, while to give the tree means allowing God to pull it up by the roots. True sacrifice goes beyond sacrificing this and that. True sacrifice is the habit of surrender. Christ's surrender to the Father's will did not begin in Gethsemani. "I do *always* the things that are pleasing to him" (Jn. 8:29).

Even the term "contemplation" should not be thought of in the way that we contemplate a sunset, still less in the way that we contemplate changing our job. It would be to restrict the meaning if mystical contemplation referred only to the act of consciously and deliberately standing before God in awe. It is taken to cover the variety of experiences between the beginning of the Illuminative Way and the crowning of the Unitive Way. It can show itself in the actual exercise of prayer but assumes such consequences of the grace as darkness, discouragement, near-despair on the one hand, and fidelity, joy, hope, confidence on the other. Contemplation is the habit of soul which desires God above all things and which trusts him absolutely in the guidance of one's life whether inward or outward. A characteristic of contemplation is the knowledge that grace alone can bring about one's sanctification. Self-sanctification is a contradictory term. Powerless to take a single step towards God without grace, the soul learns humility in contemplation. The texts in St. John which stress our human incapacity should be enough to convince us of this long before even the Purgative Way is entered upon, but it is in the Illuminative and Unitive Ways that their truth is borne home. "No one can receive anything unless it is given to him from heaven" (Jn. 3:27). "It is the spirit that gives life, the flesh profits nothing" (Jn. 6:63). Especially directed towards souls of prayer are our Lord's words: "Every branch that bears fruit he will prune, that it may bear more fruit... abide in me, and I in you. As the branch cannot bear fruit of itself unless it remain on the vine, so neither can you unless you abide in me... without me you can do nothing" (Jn. 15:2, 4-5).

The great mistake that the Pharisees made in our Lord's time was that they thought they could do something. They were not evil men, or even for the most part conscious hypocrites. They were following their vocation: they were strict observers of the law, they fasted, prayed, gave to the poor, studied, and furthered education. The only thing they left out was the element of grace. They thought they could raise themselves to heaven by pulling on their sandal-straps. To them heaven depended upon their goodness and not upon God's. Their very virtues, or rather virtuous practices, got in the way of their service of God. The Liturgy in the Temple was probably at the highest peak in its history but because the priests missed its inward significance and trusted in its excellent performance they could not see what it meant or where they were going wrong. The Pharisees and priests were intent upon piling up merit before God and were forgetting from whom all merit comes. God rewards only his own works, and there is no merit apart from him. All good comes from him and must go back to him. Mary knew this when she said in the *Magnificat*: "He has looked upon the lowliness of his handmaid. . . he who is mighty has done great things for me" (Lk. 1:49). St. Paul too knew his own nothingness: "By the grace of God I am what I am, and his grace in me has not been void" (1 Cor. 15:10).

If the Pharisees and priests had been given to interior prayer they would have come to know their true state. The Illuminative Way shows up our baseness, corruption, falseness. Either we bounce away from what we see and try to forget it, making excuses, or we face our loathsomeness and hand ourselves over to the mercy of God. To take the first course is to put off any advance in the spiritual life, to take the second is to learn dependence on God and humility.

Still on the subject of terms, there is a distinction between contemplation and the contemplative life. The life of "contemplation" implies a way of prayer in which God is the primary agent. The "contemplative life" is the exterior state of withdrawal from the world normally associated with enclosed religious orders. There can be contemplatives who are engaged in active work, and certainly not all who are living the contemplative life are contemplatives. It is not here a question of labels but of interior prayer. It is because many like to be thought of as contemplatives, when in fact they are not, that the distinction is made. If everyone prayed according to the grace God gives him nobody would have to bother about whether he was an active or contemplative soul. In the prayer life, as in any other, it is possible to be a snob. The professional contemplative is no better than the professional Pharisee.

How is the transition from the Purgative to the Illuminative Way effected, from what might be called natural to supernatural activity? And is the taking over appreciated at the time? Since God is the prime agent in each of the soul's changes along the way it would be rash to give clear-cut answers to any of the questions which come up in accounting for spiritual progress, but so long as the words "normal experience" are understood with this in mind there is no harm in generalizing. Given God's free gift of grace, then, the soul's reaction to the first light of the Illuminative Way will largely depend on three factors: natural temperament, generosity in cooperation, opportunity of securing solitude and silence in which to respond to the attraction of interior prayer.

One generalization which it would be rash to make would be to claim that the soul is always conscious of having passed from the Purgative to the Illuminative Way. Thus some can be practicing contemplation for months or years before they recognize the grace that has been given them; others come to contemplative prayer by way of sudden realization. Both processes are evident in the reply given by a nineteenth century Byzantine monk when asked how his state had been arrived at. "For many years," he said, "I was carrying prayer in my heart but did not know it. It was like a spring of water covered by a stone. Then Jesus took the stone away." Whichever way you look at it, the initiation is brought about by God. It is a culmination, a reward not merited but legitimately aspired to. The dawn may come gradually, allowing the soul to look back and see what has been going on, or it may take the soul by surprise. Jesus does not pledge himself to "take the stone away" overnight. But whenever he does, the soul is aware that the situation has changed. The first night is over, and such is the joy of having come out of it that from now on the way is felt to be clear and full of light. If other nights are to follow, and according to the books they will, they are not immediately envisaged or feared. The future is left confidently in God's hands, and for the present let the daylight be made the most of and gratefully enjoyed.

To illustrate the differing processes by which souls arrive at the first experience of infused contemplation, two letters may be quoted. The first is from a mature religious, a member of a contemplative order and in perpetual vows. It reads:

I think it began during last year's retreat which set me off reading more and giving longer time to prayer. I can't say I noticed anything at first, but as time went by I found it getting easier to be recollected and to practice the presence of God even when working at quite distracting jobs, answering the telephone, looking after guests, and at community recreation. You know what a loner I am, well since that retreat I have come to love the sisters in a way I hadn't done before. Also (but of course this may be just the result of my reading) I am increasingly able to see the finger of God in what's going on in the affairs of the world outside—in the way things are shaping in different countries and different social classes. I can't think now why I didn't see all this before because it's simply the providence of God and ought to be obvious. It is only now I can see how difficult the years in the convent have been. I'm keeping my fingers crossed in case this is being only a lull, but at least I am happier than I have ever been and I don't have regrets about the past. That verse which comes at Matins on Thursdays (no, its at Lauds; I've looked it up), *Laetati sumus pro diebus quibus nos humiliasti, annis quibus vidimus mala,* I can now say truthfully. I don't think I had noticed it before, or if I had I doubt if I meant it. Also when our Lord said, "My peace I give to you," I can now see how literally he meant it. It is his and not mine. Or rather, because he has given it to me it is mine to share with his. If there is any delusion in what I have written in this letter you must tell me frankly. The last thing I want is to be guided by imagination and not by truth.

Compare the above to a letter written by a young monk not yet in final vows and belonging to an active community.

I didn't write about this at once because I wanted to be sure that I wasn't making it up, and adding details as I went along. Now that it's a week since it happened I feel I can make a calm judgment. Well, I was praying in front of the tabernacle after tea, meaning to stay there for half an hour, and in no time the bell was ringing for Vespers. I had been there for two hours and it had felt like forty minutes at the most. If it hadn't been for Vespers I would have been quite glad to stay on. Nothing that one reads about in books as sometimes happening physically—feeling numb or hot or breathing differently—took place. It was just that I felt at ease and not under any strain. Usually when I pray I am making frantic efforts and making sure that I am praying properly, but this time it all seemed to be flowing naturally and all I had to do was to let it. In fact, looking back, freedom seems to have been the chief emotion. Except that "emotion" is the wrong word because I didn't feel excited in any way. "Sensation" would be the wrong word too, but certainly there was a *sense* of freedom. Freedom and calm. It was the sort of feeling you get when you have been given an injection before an operation—all is well and you don't mind what happens. Later, during Vespers, it was like floating through the psalms and understanding them better at the same time. Coming out in procession at the end of Vespers was as if I was seeing the brethren for the first time as they really are, and this made me feel very warmly towards them. I hoped they were seeing me in the same way. This sense of community may have weakened a bit during the week but it is still there and should be a great help from the practical point of view. Other things I have noticed too since that day: a better understanding of Scripture, a greater dependence on God and his providential will—whether he wants me to go on to profession or not, whether I shall be kept on in my present job, whether my parents will be coming to see me. A number of things like that. As regards my usual temptations and sins, I see them to be as shameful as ever but I trust more in grace and mercy. I am culpable and penitent but no longer obsessed by guilt. Loving confidence has not altogether taken away my guilt obsession but has made me realize how it is not as all-important as I thought it was. Fear too has been pushed into the background. I think it is all part of the new freedom. I am not afraid of praying badly, and instead of feeling cramped by rules and duties in the house I think from now onwards I shall see the point of them more and how they can help from day to day. If you tell me I am on the wrong course I shall believe you, and go back to discursive prayer and start again. I don't think I am on the wrong course—partly because it never entered my head to force a change—but I admit I would not like to try meditation or set up a system of repeating acts of faith, hope, love, contrition, etc. Those ways of praying didn't work very well before but I feel they wouldn't work at all now. Anyway I feel perfectly at peace which is surely a good sign. I have learned a lot in a few days. I mean I have been *taught* a lot. I mean I have not been trying to acquire knowledge deliberately, but simply that light has come.

It will be seen at once that while the writer of the first letter is more cautious, the writer of the second is both more impressionable and more ready to formulate his reactions. Supernatural action is to some extent influenced, though not conditioned, by natural qualities, and though these two individuals were far from being alike they experienced much the same graces and came to much the same conclusions.

It was the manner in which the light reached them that was different. In discussing the spiritual life it is never quite safe to argue either from the general to the particular or from the particular to the general. This said, the next question to come up must receive another more or less open answer.

For how long can this state of rest and spiritual euphoria be expected to last? There is no calendar for this kind of interior education but if the neophyte is strong and generous the next night normally closes in, allowing for a twilight period when the soul goes through an on-and-off devotional state, in a matter of months. To cling too tenaciously to the memory of the initiation, and to encourage a repetition, would delay the grace of darkness perhaps for years. A director who has been through the stages himself will be of great help here, explaining to the subject that what is important about the bestowal of grace during these changes is the effect it has beneath the surface. Emotional awareness of the working of grace is a valid indication as far as it goes, and is certainly not to be despised, but it should be understood that the senses register only just so far and that it is the deep down penetration which is the essence of the operation. The obvious comparison is the lamp recommended for the relief of various bodily ills. Because detachment in this matter of "sensible devotion" is so vital to spiritual progress—at any stage but especially in the early stages of the Illuminative Way—a long passage from St. John of the Cross may be quoted here.

> The time has now come to treat of the fourth and last kind of intellectual apprehensions which, as we have said, may enter the understanding by way of *spiritual feelings* which are often produced in the souls of spiritual persons. These distinct feelings may be of two kinds. Those of the first kind reside in the affection of the will, while those of the second reside in the substance of the soul...these spiritual feelings—to the extent that they are feelings only—pertain not to the understanding but to the will (and thus I do not propose to discuss them here at length; I shall treat of them in Book Three, in the course of the discussion of the night and purgation of the will). But since in the majority of cases apprehensions and intellectual knowledge overflow from these feelings to the understanding, they should at least be mentioned here...just as the spiritual feelings

which we have described are wrought in the soul passively, and thus without any effective activity on the part of the soul in bringing about their infusion, so also is the knowledge of them received in the understanding passively, that is, in such a way that the understanding plays no part in the acquisition of this knowledge. The understanding therefore, in order not to go astray and impede the benefits which come from these feelings, must do nothing with respect to them, *but must remain passive and make no use of its natural capacity.* For human nature is unable to attain to this most delicate knowledge by its own efforts, but only by keeping itself open and receptive to its influx. Let the soul therefore be resigned, humble, and passive, for, since it receives this knowledge from God passively, he, God, will communicate it whenever it pleases him, provided he finds the soul humble and detached.[2]

So what is to be the procedure during this happy interlude? If there are pitfalls to be avoided at every stage, and the further along the road the deeper the pitfalls, the two into which souls most commonly fall are self-assurance and exploiting the new-found liberty. Self-assurance is only another word for pride, and pride comes into almost everything we do. It will be noticed that in the final paragraph of the quotation from St. John of the Cross the word "humble" occurs twice. The saint knew the danger of the beginner counting himself among the elect. "At last I recognize the signs. . . it is all in the books but I couldn't see them at the time. . . I am well on the way to mystical union." Anyone who compares his present fortunate state with his former unsatisfactory one will be inclined to take a certain credit for the change. If not corrected, this self-congratulation could easily lead to a patronizing attitude towards those less blessed. To indulge the itch of superiority— "thank heaven I'm not one of the meditation-and-rosary people any more"—is the surest way to bring progress in prayer to a stop. Perhaps you have outgrown meditation, but it will do your prayer no harm to meditate for a while on some verses of the *Magnificat.* "He who is mighty has done great things for me. . . he has exalted the lowly. . . he has filled the hungry with good things." Whatever has been brought about in you has been done by him. St. John of the Cross is emphatic on the need to attribute nothing to personal merit.

[2] *Ascent to Mount Carmel,* ch. 32.

These favors do not depend on any good works performed by the soul, nor upon its meditations, although both these things tend to dispose the soul for them. But God grants these favors to whom he wills and for whatever reason he wills. It may happen that a person will have performed many good works and yet he will not be granted these touches of divine favor; and another will have done fewer and will receive them in greater abundance.[3]

Equally destructive can be the other danger, namely overplaying the sense of freedom. The trouble about discarding restraints and devotional practices is that it is difficult to know where to stop. One can all too easily become scornful of safeguards which may not be dispensed with. Silence, for instance, and self-denial. The grace of entering upon the Illuminative Way does not give a person a free run with imperfection or entitle him to shed the discipline to which he has been trained. People are like populations—they hanker for freedom and when they have got it they deteriorate. The mystical life cannot afford to jetison the ascetical life, and when mortification goes out of the window independence and indulgence come in. Immature souls—and they are still beginners at the stage we are dealing with—are prone to singularity and eccentricity. Singularity and eccentricity are relatively harmless, but when the cause is superior knowledge they are not at all so harmless—especially when the knowledge is a matter of the spirit. While regulations and observances can be smothering to the soul, the claim to liberty of spirit has to be approached with caution.

[3]*Ibid.*

CHAPTER 3
Doubt and Desperation

PSYCHIATRISTS ARE ALWAYS TELLING US that arrogance and fear go together. Rather than appear timid, a man will put on an assertive manner. We are forever compensating in one way or another for weaknesses of which we are ashamed, and during these transition stages in the spiritual life the weaknesses are under the microscope. So the twin defects of fear and overconfidence will be examined here. When the first feeling of freedom begins to ebb away, the soul has need to lean more than ever on God or he will be swept away by the current. St. Thérèse of Lisieux knew this when she wrote that "the only security lay in recognizing one's nothingness, expecting everything from the good God... not attributing to oneself the virtues that one practices, as if believing oneself capable of achieving something, but recognizing that God puts the treasure into the hands of his little ones." Yet the fear remains and it has to be faced. Neither bluster nor escape into one's loneliness will be the slightest use. None of this should be surprising when we consider what has been happening up to now. There has been the initial taste of novelty with its gestures, sincerely meant, of generosity. There has been the night of the senses successfully endured. There has been the dawn which has outshone the brightness of earlier satisfactions. Psychologically, let alone spiritually, a reaction was bound to set in. The reaction takes the form of doubt which mounts to dread, which in turn mounts to panic.

The specific doubt shows itself in a mixture of misgiving and deflected humility. "How could I have been such a fool as to think I could carry it off? It was a delusion from the start. The joys amounted to no more than the novice's first fervor; the darknesses had nothing to do with the action of God but were simply made up of the boredom, loneliness, and frustration which people suffer when they find themselves following the wrong vocation. Whatever my lofty aspirations I am clearly not cut out for this. Self-deception and not grace has brought me to my present state, and now what I dread is having to face a lifetime of not knowing where I am or who I am." It is the same old treadmill: self-doubt, doubt of God's purpose or protection, doubt of the value of everything and especially of the value of serving God in the interior life.

Apart from the fact that so much inward looking is always a mistake, there is the significant lack of dependence on God's providence which is the first necessity the whole way through. Looking back and trying to account for one's motives, trying to read one's conscience at the different stages of the course, seeing only too clearly one's present hypocrisy and increasing ill temper, bitterness, resentment can bring the soul to the edge of despair. Mention has been made earlier of what a trial the awareness of one's loathsomeness can be. Here it is not a flashlight glimpse but a punishing and constant glare. It is like living without eyelids under the beam of an arc lamp.

There is the story of a man who possessed a fine voice and who came with his girl to the mouth of a deep dry well. Without his knowing it there were snakes at the bottom of the well, hissing, spitting and writhing. "Listen while I sing down this well," he said, showing off, "and you will hear my fine voice not once but twice." So he bent over the parapet and filled the air with sound and song. But the echo which came up the shaft was harsh and discordant, full of words of obscenity and horror. What the lady thought of it is not the point—the point is what he did.

The truth about ourselves is normally so deep that we fail to see it. In the nights of sense and spirit we come to see what we really are, and if the resulting disgust does not lead to dependence on God it leads to desperation. Even more serious than desperation is despair. When panic smothers trust in God, when the only escape is felt to be death and when that too is feared on account of having to face God with nothing but failure to show for his gift of life, only the light of grace can save the situation. But if the soul hangs on, light does come. Now is the time for the ninetieth psalm: "He who dwells in the shelter of the Most High and abides in the shade of the Almighty, and says to the Lord 'my refuge, my stronghold, my God in whom I trust.' It is he who will free you from the snare...under his wings you will find refuge ...you will not fear the terror of the night." The trust will eclipse the terror, and the hope which was deadened for awhile will revive. "The scourge may lay waste at noon"—noon following noon as night follows night in the spiritual life—but though thousands may neglect the grace that is being given to you, for you he must always be counted upon as buckler and shield. His protection is there for the asking. At any moment of your life you can say, "Lord, my refuge," and can "make the Most High your dwelling."

In Arizona, and also in parts of Mexico, there is a cactus called "nightflowering." While most plants thrive in the day, this cactus needs darkness if it is to produce what God intends it to produce. If the cactus could speak, it would probably tell you that the nights in the desert were long and painful and that but for its natural limitation it would flower more abundantly during the daytime. Furthermore if you attribute to the cactus good sense, as well as the power of speech, you might hear it say, "Since of course God made me, and knows what he is about, I must go by what he has arranged for my particular kind. It is never wise to think one knows better than the person responsible."

If the sight of our sins and unworthiness is to bear fruit it must be guarded against not only the tendency to despair but also against the attitude which says there is nothing that can be done about it. There is much that can be done about it. Penance, for instance. To belittle the value of penance is one of the misconceptions to which interior souls are particularly liable. "My contemplation assumes penance." An incautious assumption. This is not the place to say what penances are suitable to souls as they advance along the way of prayer, but self-denial of some sort is—as set forth in our Lord's teaching—essential to the contemplative life.

From Origen in the third century to Rasputin in the twentieth, erroneous theologians and false mystics have glossed over the guilt of sin by putting it in the framework of God's loving providence. "Even in our sins," wrote Origen, "certain traces are retained of the divine purpose." The *pecca fortiter* idea was derived from the false understanding of St. Augustine's "love and do what you will," while the determinists of the sixteenth century were as strong about the inevitability of sin as they were about the inevitability of God's mercy. But the Russian, with his crazily warped theology, carried the theory further than anybody with his conclusion that the only way of experiencing and being grateful for God's mercy was to sin on a grand scale and to go right on sinning.

It is a curious fact that along with the consciousness of one's utter wretchedness goes at the very back of one's mind an obscure longing to realize the purpose of one's existence. Ultimately of course this is the longing for God. The nights may black out all sense of hope, and loss of direction and destination is uppermost in the mind, but there is nevertheless the vague feeling that if circumstances were different— how different and in what way is not specified—a happier condition could be achieved. The quest for God is so basic to man's nature that, and thank God for it, no darkness of faith can altogether eliminate it. "My God, my God, why have you forsaken me?" to be followed immediately by "into your hands I commend my spirit." As St. Augustine points out in what is perhaps the most famous of his sayings, man's heart is restless unless it finds rest in God. And, if only subconsciously, man knows it.[1]

Self-loathing has been treated here not so as to hold the mirror to self and increase the loathing even more. The purpose has been to raise self-loathing to self-acceptance. To stop short at self-loathing not only discourages effort, and, as we have seen, diminishes hope, but

[1]In a passage which I copied out some time ago but which I cannot now trace for reference, St. Augustine backs up his statement about finding rest only in God with these words: "Imagine God saying to you, 'I will make you a bargain. Anything and everything you ask I will give to you: pleasure, power, honor, wealth, freedom, even peace of mind and a good conscience. Nothing will be a sin, so you will feel no guilt, and nothing will be forbidden. Nothing will be impossible to you. You will never feel weary and you will never die. *Only you shall never see my face.*'" St. Augustine is not posing this test to saints and mystics but to everyone. The challenge shows us all that beyond our human appetites the appetite for union with God is the most fundamental. The passage teaches the difference between relative and absolute happiness.

inhibits prayer. Prayer should be self-forgetful absorption in God. When prayer becomes an exercise in self-analysis, or in prayer-analysis, it is being conducted on the psychiatric couch and only indirectly in the presence of God. It is good to know one's nothingness but bad not to accept it. "How happy I am to find myself so imperfect," wrote St. Thérèse of Lisieux shortly before her death, "and so much in need of God's mercy when the time comes for me to die."[2] Not excusing our failure, prayer should leave us resigned to it. Provided we are where God wants us to be we have nothing to worry about. Not wallowing in our unfitness for the spiritual life but not resentful either at having to occupy the lowest place until God gives us the grace to occupy a higher one. There is a morbid streak in most of us which likes to think we are spiritually handicapped, and we can even choose to remain so when the cure is ours for the taking. There was something of this even in St. Peter when he said, "Leave me Lord, for I am a sinful man" (Lk. 5:8). What he should have said was, "Come close to me, Lord, for I am a sinful man," but St. Peter was always getting things wrong. As Frank Sheed points out, when commenting on this incident, it would be like saying to a doctor, "Please go away, can't you see I'm sick."[3]

What we have to remember during all these trials, whether they happen to be the spiritual trials of the dark nights or the more outward trials of ordinary experience, is the truth of the psalmist's verse "it was good for me to have to suffer, the better to learn your ways" (Ps. 118:71). The Latin has *quia humiliasti me* which is nearer to what we have been considering. There is nothing so humiliating as seeing our faults, past and present, and not being able to do anything about them. If feeling abandoned by God is the worst of the contemplative's sufferings, the sense of suffering so badly runs a close second. Not until the soul is admitted to the grace of the Unitive Way, when the intellectual and emotional faculties are caught up in God, is preoccupation quite sublimated. By then the knowledge and experience of God has suspended all other interests. This will appear in a later chapter. Meanwhile in the illuminative state, for as long as self-awareness with

[2]*Derniers Entretiens*, 29.
[3]*Christ in Eclipse*, p. 13.

its accompanying anxieties and distractions lasts, there is no true or lasting peace.

Pascal records in his *Memorial* what might be called a breakthrough of the spirit, which, if the experience was temporary in its effects, could belong to the latter part of the Illuminative Way. If the peace and certainty he refers to turned out to be a settled habit it marks the end of the dark night of the soul and the dawn of the Unitive Way. Whatever the stage, the occurrence certainly relates to the mystical state. "The year of grace 1654, Monday the twenty-third of November, St. Clement's Day," wrote Pascal—and by being so precise he showed what importance he attached to the declaration which was not just another reminiscence to be included in an autobiography—"from about half-past ten in the evening until about half an hour past midnight—fire. God of Abraham. God of Isaac. God of Jacob. Not God of the philosophers and the learned. Certainty. Certainty. Feeling, joy, peace. Forgetfulness of the world and of everything other than God."[4] If according to the categories the placing of the event is debatable, at least it favors the "big bang" manner of initiation as distinct from the gradual evolution. After his death some of the words of the above deposition were found written out and sewn into one of Pascal's pockets. "Certainty, certainty. Feeling, joy, peace."

In the light of what Pascal says about fire, it is interesting to see how St. Teresa associates the beginning of infused contemplation with fire. "Water which springs from the earth," she says,

> has no power over this fire. Its flames rise high and its source is in nothing so base as the earth. There are other fires of love for God—small ones which may be quenched by the least little thing. But this fire—no, no. Even if a whole sea of temptations assail it, they will not keep it from burning or prevent it from gaining mastery over them...nothing worldly has warmth enough left in it to induce us to cling to it unless it is something which increases this fire, the nature of which is not to be easily satisfied, but if possible to enkindle the whole world.[5]

In the same chapter, and while still speaking of the interaction

---

[4]Bremond, *Histoire Littéraire du Sentiment Religieux en France*, vol. IV, p. 359.
[5]*The Way of Perfection*, ch. 19.

between fire and water in the soul's hunger for God, St. Teresa makes it clear that even in these advanced states of prayer there will still be distractions to worry about.

> Almost without noticing it, we find ourselves ruminating on things in the world that we love. We try to banish these thoughts but we cannot help being slightly distracted by thinking of things that have happened, or will happen, of things we have done and of things we are going to do. Then we begin to wonder how we can get rid of these thoughts; and that sometimes plunges us again into the same danger. It is not that we ought to omit such preoccupations but that we need to retain our misgivings about them and not to grow careless. In contemplation the Lord Himself relieves us of this care, for He will not trust us to look after ourselves. So dearly does He love us that He prevents us from rushing into things which may do us harm just at this time when He is anxious to help us. . . in contemplation the Lord brings us to the end of the day's journey without our understanding how.[6]

The obstacles to pure contemplation which St. Teresa is referring to here, namely memories and anxieties, are not the desperations experienced in the Illuminative Way nor the desolations of the dark night of the soul. They are the distractions of every day which beset us all, the wanderings of the mind and the wayward imaginations; they are not to be taken too seriously. We only aggravate distractions by concentrating on them and by making violent efforts to suppress them. To try to smack down troubled water with a tennis racket only adds other waves. To apply the brake too forcefully can prevent the car from starting up again. Not all evils, whether temptations outside prayer time or idle meandering reveries while praying, are disposed of by direct confrontation. When our Lord said, "resist not evil" (Mt. 5:39), he was not telling us to let evil have its way but, from the examples he chose, was showing us that evil can only be overcome by good, by love. Frequently we come across reformers, spiritual directors, educators, politicians, who think that by getting rid of everything that contains the seeds of destruction or opposition they can ensure the ideal they are aiming at. All they do is to produce a void, an area of waste which might have been productive. Our Lord taught this with the parable of the wheat

---

[6]*Ibid.*

and the cockle (Mt. 13:29). *Ubi solitudinem faciunt, pacem appellant,* wrote Tacitus, "when they made a desert, they called it peace." Love is not created by eliminating hate; love is created by love. Just as perfect love casts out fear, perfect humility casts out pride. If the roots of fear and the roots of pride remain, the fruits of fear and the fruits of pride are cut off. By analogy it might further be said that perfect peace casts out anxiety, discord, nerves. But there is room for misapprehension here because peace must be understood as Christ's peace, the positive peace of the Spirit which resides in the will and not the negative peace which is brought about by careful planning. Gandhi is reputed to have said, "I do not want the peace of a stone"; there is nothing more supine than a stone.

There is all the difference between self-sufficiency and acceptance. All the difference too between acceptance in faith and acceptance in the spirit of fatalism. There is only one way to peace and that is acceptance. There is only one way to acceptance and that is to learn it in prayer from Christ. Outward peace, the kind we arrive at by forethought and circumspection, is well worth having but it is the inward peace which the Illuminative Way brings about without our having to strive after it that marks the beginning of infused contemplation. This latter peace is the kind mentioned in the quotation from Pascal. Such peace is enjoyed intermittently, and for long periods of time, in the Illuminative Way; in the Unitive Way it is a settled habit. Those who are enduring the trials of the dark nights, even during the tribulations described earlier in this chapter, would admit that because they have, however dimly, accepted God's handling of their souls, a certain indefinable peace is present. The very act of offering one's tribulations to God, unworthily and even reluctantly endured, brings at least the gratification of having nothing else, nothing better to offer. All one's inadequacies are handed over; the more one is made aware of them the more one wants to hand them over. Not that at this stage the motive is pure—because the first desire is to get rid of them and not to have to think about them—but there is faith of a sort acting here, and where there is any degree of faith there must be some degree of acceptance. "The acceptance of oneself," wrote Jung, "is the essence of the moral problem and the epitome of a whole outlook upon life...

what I do unto the least of my brethren, that I do unto Christ. But what if I should discover that the least among them all, the poorest of all the beggars, the most impudent of all offenders, the very enemy himself—that these are within me and that I myself stand in need of the alms of my own kindness—that I myself am the enemy who must be loved—what then?"[7] In giving this quotation, Alan Watts adds, "in short, therefore, self-loathing must give place to self-acceptance, which is permitting oneself to be loved by God."[8]

The doctrine of de Caussade, best expressed in his *Abandonment to the Divine Providence*, is putting the doctrine of Zen and the philosophy of Mahayana Buddhism in a Christian context and is particularly appropriate to the experience of the dark nights and the Illuminative Way. When we read in Dionysius of the "hid divinity" and the "luminous darkness," the Areopagite was describing, whether he knew it or not, what Chinese Buddhism would call the search for Reality and Enlightenment which had been going on for centuries in the religions of the East. Even some of the images used in the literature of eastern mysticism are paralleled in ours of the West. The Buddhist "pregnant void" could be matched by the Christian "active receptivity," "divine darkness," "cloud of unknowing," "cloud of forgetting," and so on. Where a misunderstanding of de Caussade could lead to Quietism, a right understanding of his "abondonment" leads to the acceptance of Mary's "be it done unto me according to your word" and Christ's "not my will but yours be done."

So to sum up, the more there is of self-acceptance the less there is of self-absorption. Awareness of God replaces awareness of self. "Except to humiliate oneself and love our Lord, one should never dwell upon oneself or one's offenses," wrote Père de Condren the Oratorian, and it is only logical that where one is one's main interest, God inevitably takes second place. Contemplation restores the right order. If contem-

---

[7] *Modern Man in Search of a Soul*, pp. 271-272. Quoted by Alan Watts in *Behold the Spirit*, p. 211.
[8] *Behold the Spirit*, p. 211.

plation shows us what we are, it also shows us what we might be if we made use of the graces God gives us.

There was once a king who gave a great feast for the noblest in the land, and at the entrance to the banquet hall he had placed a tall framed looking glass which the guests would have to pass before being shown to their places at the tables. The looking glass possessed this property, that all who looked in it could see themselves as they truly were. The guests, faced with their reflections in the mirror and blushing for shame, hurried past the great mirror into the banquet hall hoping that in the consumption of food and drink they would forget what they had seen, and hoping too that their fellow guests were likewise so shocked by the sight of their true selves as to leave no room in their minds for the observation of what was revealed to any but themselves. Last to arrive, fashionably late so as to make an impressive entry, came the most important guest of the evening, a man respected by all for his virtue and integrity, rich, handsome, and occupying the highest place in the realm after the king, well-born and proper in his bearing. This man, pausing in front of the mirror to assure himself of his appearance, was so incensed by what he saw that he smashed the cruel glass of truth into a thousand pieces. "They shall not see this travesty," he cried and went home in a mood of puffed ill-temper. But this was not the end of it, for the guests, somewhat mellowed and having toasted the king as the most generous of hosts, were now no longer so conscious of their embarrassment as they passed out of the great chamber to see on the floor the countless pieces of broken mirror. Relief filled their hearts since there was now little chance of being exposed in public for what they really were. But this time each one saw in his separate piece of glass the kind of person he could have been. And this was an even more shaming revelation than the earlier one.

CHAPTER 4
Varied Progress

WE HAVE NOW SEEN how God has taken the soul at its word when the total surrender was made at the beginning. In the active night of sense the main work of grace was to stiffen the soul's resolution and train the will. In the passive night of sense the soul's offer to God of memory, imagination, the emotions, and the body has been accepted, but not to the soul's satisfaction. God is doing the teaching and the soul, with whatever difficulty, is learning. Contemplation, even at this stage when the soul is practicing the prayer of simplicity—or feeling drawn to it though not altogether convinced of its validity as compared with the discursive prayer of before—is a receptive and not a contributory act. The prayer of simplicity puts no strain on the head and can be continued for longer stretches of time than the prayer of forced acts or spontaneously expressed affections. But even the prayer of simplicity requires effort; it is not just free-wheeling with the lights on through the twilight hour. The beginner, and all are beginners until infused grace has eclipsed the soul's natural industry, has to prove himself. As always it is the test of faith and perseverance. The testing brings the soul to deeper levels of experience, to more searching exposures of weakness. Preparation for entry upon the Unitive Way is the action of grace eliciting from the soul the willingness to be worked upon by God in any way that he may choose. This drawn out submission is both the primary condition for future graces and the habitual disposition. This is the passive dark night of the soul, and since the softening-up process which is the introduction to union normally lasts a long time and also because it defies step-by-step measurement, the next few chapters will indicate some of the features which accompany it.

The texts to remember while reading of these nights with their trials, still more while experiencing them, are from our Lord's own lips. "My God, my God, why have you forsaken me" (Mk. 15:34), followed by "it is finished" (Jn. 19:30) (more accurately "it is achieved" which means more than bringing to an end; it means "it has been brought about as planned"), followed in turn by "it is expedient that I go, for if I do not go the Paraclete will not come to you" (Jn. 16:7). This is the lesson of the dark nights: we lose him at one level so that we may find him at another. Our human knowledge of him gives place to the spiritual knowledge. After the Resurrection, "he appeared to them in another form" (Mk. 16:12), and it is in this new form that we are being taught to look for him.

The attempt to chart the course of spiritual development can never hope to apply to more than a narrow majority of souls. This said, and granted that no two souls are alike, there do exist, nevertheless, general guidelines and it would be rash to jump them. Our Lord has said, "I am the way, and no man comes to the Father except by me" (Jn. 14:6), but each soul's discovery of the way, as each soul's experience along the way, will be unique. The Good Shepherd draws the flock of sheep towards himself, yet each individual sheep responds to him in its own way. There are hireling shepherds, today more than ever before, who, in the name of greater liberty, are scornful of categories and demarkations. Our Lord was not. "In my Father's house there are many mansions" (Jn. 14:2). You cannot have mansions without walls and staircases, and any director who imagines he can convey souls by elevator from the ground floor to the rooftop penthouse without bothering about the floors on the way up will be no help to the passengers. This does not mean that the soul must study the gradations and assure himself that he has arrived at the right landing. It means that when there is felt to be no upward movement, and this is the normal condition of the soul after leaving the active night of sense, there are at least the authorities to fall back upon. The reason why St. John of the Cross is chosen here, and not for instance St. Augustine or St. Teresa, is because his thought can be followed. He writes in the manner of a trained theologian, which he was, rather than with the free association technique which is popular today. Among the many other writers who cover the same ground, the names of Arintero, Poulain, Garrigou-Lagrange suggest themselves. Their works will, in the nature of the case, be more helpful to the director than the directed. The directed will not get much help from any written work apart perhaps from the Psalms, the Book of Job, and the Gospels.

If readers of St. John's books find him forbidding, especially in the case of *The Ascent of Mount Carmel* and *The Dark Night of the Soul,* it is because they have given more attention to the trials he describes than to the doctrine as a whole. Taken by themselves the trials might seem discouraging but since the overall theme is God's merciful love, at each stage drawing the timid soul by the strength of grace, there is nothing of which the beginner need be afraid. The only thing about his writing which could lead to fear would be the mistake of looking to see if one's current experience is conforming to the pattern as laid down in the book. So it is worth repeating here that self-examination is the enemy of trust, and that advance and delay in the spiritual life are occasioned to the degree of, respectively, trust and self-absorption which sees God in the soul.

For St. John of the Cross the soul's giving in to the unrestricted action of grace is the whole story. The response has to be freely given; the action of grace is not tied down. The Holy Spirit does not pledge himself to fall in with a particular *schema* or schedule of time. To read St. John of the Cross with any profit the beginner must realize that God acts as freely as he does. Not that God should be allowed to act on impulse but that God should be allowed to act according to laws of his own about which we know little. His communication with the soul is secret. We cannot argue from our own ways of acting that God acts in the same way. We can sometimes—as when the Lord says in Isaias, "Can a woman forget her own child...yet even if she forget I will never forget you" (Is. 49:15)—not always however because, "My thoughts are not your thoughts, my ways are not your ways. It is the Lord who speaks" (Is. 55:8). It is for the director to use his God-given gift of discernment in deciding what place in the spiritual life his penitent is occupying and what normally speaking will be the next step. Without some knowledge of the mystics, and especially of St. John of the Cross, he will be likely to keep the beginner stuck forever in the active night of sense.[1] Enlightened directors are not easy to come by, as St. Teresa frequently admits, but even without a director the beginner can get along on the strength of a generous intention of developing, according to his opportunity, the life of prayer. The same generous intention of practicing mortification, according to circumstances and prudent judgment, will, in St. Teresa's opinion, ensure direction from God. Later on, when doubts appear as to the validity of his experience, and when he feels he should be praying differently but does not know how to go about it, the beginner will need to consult someone who is more advanced, and he will also learn from books, but for the time being he may safely rely on what he truly believes to be the promptings of grace. By then he will not be a beginner anyway.

This might be the place, after so much has been said about prayer, to treat of mortification. Penance as well as penance*s*, which is not quite the same thing, is a subject much overlooked in present day religious practice. At one time the balance between ascetic and mystical commitment was understood, and the value given to each was taught. Not so now. Granted that prayer is more important than penance, because it unites the soul more directly and intimately to God, penance is nevertheless an essential element in the spiritual life. Penance, rightly handled, *is* prayer. Penances should rise up to God on the impulse of prayer and joined with it. To give the whole emphasis to prayer to the exclusion of penance is not only to upset the balance but to turn the prayer into an aesthetic exercise, a culture. Prayer and penance together make up an *ascesis*. If prayer without penance is for the dilettante, penance without prayer is for the fakir and the flagellant.

Most of those who would not dream of finding excuses to avoid prayer are adept at finding excuses for getting out of penance. "I'm not attracted to it as I am to prayer." "I don't find it does me any good."

---

[1]Again when we talk of "beginners" we are not thinking of the child learning the *Our Father* but of the soul who has passed through the first nights and who is floundering about in the Illuminative Way. This is the time when he will need direction. He will need to be reassured that his call to contemplation has not been a delusion. On the practical side he will need to be guided as to how much time he should give to mental prayer, and as to what mortification he should practice.

"People who fast a lot are so disagreeable." "I feel if I pray more I can make up for not doing penance." "After all I am not now committing the kinds of sins which require penance." It is not only sinners who are expected to be penitent. If penance were required of the guilty only, why would the most innocent of saints be so often noted for their penances. In the vision granted to the Prophet Zacharias five centuries before Christ, the suffering Messiah was shown standing in the Temple and showing the wounds in his hands and feet. "With these I was wounded," the sufferer explains, "in the house of my friends" (13:6). Not in the house of my enemies but in the house of those who loved me—but not enough. This comes after an earlier passage in which the question is asked, "Ought I to go on mourning and fasting in the fifth month as I have been doing for so many years past?" (7:3).

It should shame us to see how many sacrifices are made for indifferent and even unworthy and sinful causes when the call to make sacrifices for the love of God is evaded. No list of penitential exercises suitable to those in this or that mansion, in this or that dark night, will be given here. This is something which will be determined by a number of factors such as obedience, opportunity, health, personal interior attraction, but while mortifications are not the whole of penance, mortification of self, body as well as intellect and will, is certainly required by God. That this is less and less recognized in our libertarian society can only do harm to spirituality. A noted Dominican, Fr. John Krenzke, has said: "It is a popular but untrue idea that when we do something physically hard it is therefore meritorious before God." If it is done with the right intention it is obviously meritorious. "It may be for example," the same writer goes on to say, "very difficult to give up smoking during Lent (or at any other time) but there is no spiritual growth as such in the act of giving up smoking. All too often the reason for Lent is thought of as a time to do hard things in order to do penance for our sins."[2] Well, isn't it? Otherwise what is Lent for?

More significant is the dropping, in the Jerusalem Bible, of the last two words from our Lord's statement, "This kind of devil can be cast

---

[2]*Denver Catholic Register*, February 4, 1981.

out only by prayer *and fasting*" (Mk. 9:29). A lot of exegetical justification must account for this. Fasting may not claim too much for itself by the side of praying but at least it is a pledge of good faith, a token offering, an accepted earnest of sufferings to come. In the covenant between God and man, and especially in the covenant between God and would-be contemplative man, love is the main exchange. The appropriate expression of love, on man's part as on Christ's, is sacrifice. Where denial of the flesh is looked upon as an anachronism, a fetish belonging to the Middle Ages, false mysticism is not far away. What with satanic cults on the increase and spiritualism everywhere becoming fashionable, false mysticism is anyway not far from us. It is for the astringent quality of asceticism to act as antiseptic. If mysticism is not to become a holy pastime, a down-to-earth asceticism must come to the rescue or self-indulgence will eventually bring the spiritual life to a stop.

At the beginning, back in the Purgative Way and the active dark night of the senses, the neophyte was all for denying himself, body and spirit; he found it stimulating. Nothing was too much for him to undertake for the love of God and to keep pace with the principle of total conversion. The discipline, the hairshirt, sleeping on boards, not eating—all so much evidence of the new life. "I am not fasting to keep fit or for my figure or because my mind works better; I am fasting for you, Lord, and I wouldn't be doing it for anyone else." When working at his job, whether manual or intellectual, he says, "I want this to be for your greater glory, Lord, and not to make money or because I like it or because I am told to do it." The sense of novelty and of dedication was given by God but was not appreciated as the gift of grace. I, the generous *I*, was doing the work. Precisely to correct this element of self-congratulation, along comes the passive night of the senses which at the same time hides from the soul all knowledge of what is going on so that the work of grace can operate unhindered. Out of the way is the admixture of self, malleable in its state of ignorance, the will accepting even though the emotions are protesting, the beginner is well on the way to becoming a proficient.

While he is still half-novice and half-qualified, the soul keeps on protesting that he wants only God's will and that he leaves the outcome entirely in God's hands. The soul has not the faintest idea as to what the gesture is letting him in for. "If it knew," says St. John of the Cross, "the will to go forward might be lacking." Wry humor is not normally associated with this saint.

And now, to pick up the story as we left it in the earlier stages of the Illuminative Way, we have noted how the active night of the spirit has been working on the more hidden and subtle imperfections which still linger in the soul after the passive night of sense has done as much as it could on its own level. But darkness, whether of sense or spirit, has more than a purifying part to play: it strengthens the soul's response to grace. The author of *The Cloud of Unknowing* has this to say about the course the soul should take in cooperating here:

> Cease not, therefore, but labor on this work until you feel the hunger for God alone. The first time that you try, you will find only a darkness, as though it were a cloud of unknowing which you do not understand, only that you feel in your will a naked intent unto God. Whatever you do, this darkness and this cloud is between you and God so that you do not see him either by the reasoning of your intellect or feel him in the affection of your heart. Therefore you will have no other course to follow than to stay in this darkness in the best spirit that you can, always calling upon him whom you desire.[3]

And again in the same chapter: "Lift up your heart unto God with a meek loving love, and let there be but a naked intent unto God alone and not to anything that he has made. It is this work of your soul that pleases God most."

If in the above passage the impression is given that "the meek loving love" is a matter of glowing emotion, a devotional reaction, then the term "naked intent unto God," which is a favorite expression with this author, corrects the idea. An "intent" is something willed, and the fact that it is "naked" would indicate that it is not accompanied by the sensation of loving. *The Cloud* is easier to read than St. John of the Cross, but its doctrine is no less forthright: God alone, and the only

---

[3] *The Cloud of Unknowing*, pp. 23-25.

way to know it by experience is to travel through the tunnels of darkness. It is from "unknowing" that the soul comes to know. Losing our concepts of God, which are bound to be wrong anyway, we come dimly to see his truth in the reflected light of his love. Just as looking with open eyes at the sun cannot be endured for long but only shows black spots, so looking at God produces the same result. Human vision is inadequate for the sight of God, so natural perspectives have to give place to supernatural perspectives, and for this to take place God has to adjust the focus. The process is inevitably painful to the subject. The brightness of divine light strikes darkness to the eyes that are turned towards it.

"That life was the light of men, a light that shines in the darkness, and darkness could not understand it" (Jn. 1:4-5).[4] Darkness never does until afterwards, and then it becomes light, and joy, and peace.

---

[4]*The Jerusalem Bible* renders the last sentence "a light the darkness could not overpower," which misses the point given by the Latin *comprehenderunt* (take in or grasp) and by the Greek *katelaben* (contain or assimilate). We must presume that the Hebrew, a language with which the present writer is unfamiliar, is the authority for "overpower."

CHAPTER 5
Active, Contemplative, Mixed

HOW, IT MIGHT BE ASKED, does all this interior activity square with outward responsibility? Granted that love of God comes first, but so far nothing has been said about love of neighbor. Are contemplatives above serving their fellow men? Even the most elevated mystics must surely have responsibilities towards the rest of us? For answer we turn to the champions of the mixed life, St. Gregory and St. Thomas, both of whom put the life of combined action and contemplation above that of the purely contemplative. In the quotations to be drawn upon in this chapter, indeed throughout the study of the mixed life, the words "active," "activity," "apostolic" have to be understood in a qualified sense. Neither St. Gregory nor St. Thomas would claim that the mixed life could mix with everything without loss to its contemplative side. The corporal and spiritual works of mercy are one thing; social and recreational activities, under the vague cover of making contacts with fellow members of Christ's mystical body, are another. The mixed life, if it is to rank above the contemplative life, applies its sanctions strictly. It cares for the poor and sick, it teaches and preaches, it advises and corrects; it does not meddle in secular affairs. The principle is that combining prayer with apostolic labor, the soul mounts in an ascending spiral to God who has appointed himself the final end of both. The trouble begins when the spiral collapses under the weight of active works.

You have the Curé of Ars spending many hours a day in the confessional. You have St. Peter Claver consoling and converting African slaves in the stinking holds of ships. You have St. Bernardine constantly on the move and preaching until he could no longer stand upright. Would these and thousands of others in the mixed life have found sanctity had they involved themselves in amateur theatricals, coached football teams, lectured on the history of skiing and surfing?

What if the work is of its nature secular but given under obedience—the job of cook in a community, for instance, or teacher in a school—are not such jobs sanctifying? Done with the intention of pleasing God and in virtue of obedience, they certainly are. What is submitted here is that outward works of any kind, whether self-chosen or under cover of obedience, may *if allowed to* lower the degree of union with God in prayer. It would be a mistake, indeed a form of superstition, to believe that obedience removed the likelihood of harm from indifferent or potentially harmful acts. Obedience can sanctify an act but it cannot guarantee immunity. Obedience is not magic. In one of Maupassant's stories, *L'Elixir du Frère Gauchet,* the brother who invented a new and powerful drink, and who alone held the recipe, comes to the abbot and asks if he may hand over the job of mixing and measuring the components to another. He is constantly having to taste the brew, he says, and he fears he may turn into a drunkard. The abbot tells him he has enriched the abbey and brought pleasure to many; he must go back to his still, in the knowledge that his obedience is taking care of everything. Thereafter, night after night, the abbot hears gales of drunken song and laughter coming from the brother's workshop.

That was fiction, now from fact. A monk who was professed in an extremely strict community in an extremely cloistered order was put in charge of the monastery car. This meant he was called upon to drive to the airport, to doctors and hospitals, to neighboring towns on errands of one sort or another. Not having left the enclosure for years until he was given the new assignment he found his prayer now was much distracted. He had for some time been granted the grace of infused contemplation. On representing to his superior, as he was advised to do by his director, that he needed more solitude if his prayer life were to survive, he was told that at the cost of a few distractions he was serving God and his community better than he had ever done before...obedience meant making sacrifices, and to sacrifice something spiritual when fulfilling the wishes of a superior, God's representative, was all the more meritorious and sanctifying. Meritorious it may have been, and it may even have been a dark night of sorts, but he had to drop back into the Purgative Way and begin his climb from there.

On the evidence of this account, active works not directly designed to promote prayer have the same effect on the imagination, the nerves, and the emotions as they would in the case of someone who was not trying to lead the spiritual life. The images are there whether you like it or not, and neither obedience nor the overall good intention either prevents them from entering the mind or expunges them when you put the car back in the garage. It is no compliment to the virtue of obedience to treat it as though it cast a holy spell. You do not walk into a lion's cage on the grounds that the lion was given to you by a pope. Obedience is meant to safeguard prayer, not bully it into distraction.

Having considered the mixed life in relation to obedience we can now consider the mixed life in relation to charity. Though not the same, the problems presented run parallel. Where the object of the activity is explicitly charity, the margin of confusion is narrowed. Someone has said that the only difference between the active and the contemplative apostle is that where the active speaks to people about God, the contemplative speaks to God about people. The point here is that God is the object of attention in each of them. In strictly apostolic works God is already there, helping *ex abundantia contemplationis*. In secular works he has to be called in so that what is being done can be handed back to him. While the destination is the same, the inspiration is different. If the mixed life is to qualify for first place it is the inspiration, namely the God-given gift of contemplation, which concerns us here. By "inspiration" we mean the force which gets the activity going. In the active life the motives are so numerous and mixed when undertaking a particular work that it is difficult, even for the person concerned, to tell quite what the main drive is. In the contemplative life the purposes reduce themselves to one, namely union with God for God's greater glory. In the mixed life action and contemplation come together, informing one another in such a way that the soul's prayer activity during outward performance is hardly different from what goes on during the exercise of prayer. The classical example of this is to be found in Brother Lawrence of the Trinity, a true contemplative if ever there was one, who said he no longer minded being sent on business trips because he could practice recollection while settling accounts and wheeling barrels along a warf as easily as when kneeling in choir. It helped that he was acting under obedience and not by his own choice, but the ability to live in the presence of God was a particular grace granted to him in virtue of his contemplation. His short book, *The Practice of the Presence of God,* must have helped more souls than weighty volumes on the subject of prayer. For one thing he shows, without setting out to grind an axe, that Carmelite spirituality is not the prerogative of the chosen few.

In considering the three ways of life, the active, the contemplative, and the mixed, it is a mistake to go too much by the labels. People do not as a rule set out to lead one or another. More often God leads them, according to their particular propensity, to follow one line rather than another. Man likes labels and categories (hence books like this one) but God does not pledge himself to observe accepted classifications. This is especially true in the matter of vocation, and whether a soul follows an active, contemplative, or mixed way of life depends more on grace than choice.

It is natural when thinking of Martha and Mary in the Gospel to oversimplify. Martha stands for the active life, Mary for the contemplative. But they were people before they were symbols. They are not arguments for or against this or that pattern of behavior. Not only were they people but they were sisters—both loving Jesus but not rivals in the love each was showing him. When two saints, even if they do not happen to be sisters, love our Lord before all else, they are not vying with one another in a competition of love. They are too busy with the object of their love to worry about things like manner or degree. Being "busy" does not necessarily mean being highly charged or even discernably occupied. Martha and Mary were full of love, and though on the occasion recorded in St. Luke's tenth chapter Mary's way of showing what she felt was put above Martha's more practical approach, there is nothing to show that Mary did not take her turn next day with the dishes and that Martha did not sit at our Lord's feet when she felt like it. Part active, part contemplative—each part filling in the gaps left by the other and raising the whole to the height proposed by St. Gregory and St. Thomas. It is the "naked intent unto God" that really matters, and this, by God's grace, can be arrived at wherever the labels place us.

If much of what has been said is felt to confuse and not clarify the active-contemplative-mixed issue let St. Thomas, the clearest of the Church's Doctors, be invoked here.

> The active life may be considered from two points of view. First as regards the attention to and practice of external works; and thus it is evident that the active life hinders the contemplative insofar as it is impossible for one to be busy with external action and at the same time give oneself to divine contemplation. Second, active life may be considered as quieting and directing the internal passions of the soul; and from this point of view the active life is a help to the contemplative. Hence St. Gregory says: "Those who wish to hold the fortress of contemplation must first of all train in the camp of action."[1]

There are several points to be noticed about this. St. Thomas talks about external activities having "a quieting and directing" effect upon the soul, coming in as a controlling influence on the soul's natural passions. He is suggesting that it is a good thing for the soul to have outlets. This is very much in the Dominican tradition which introduced the idea that religious orders were right to undertake apostolic work not only for the good of those whom their members were serving but even more for the members themselves. If religious orders were to spare themselves psychiatric problems, the best thing they could do would be to find some sort of apostolic work, it did not much matter what, which would satisfy the need. This is a test which might be applied not only to the contemplative religious but to the contemplative lay person. The findings would most probably result in the vocation to the mixed life.

Another point from the quotation which shows St. Thomas' mind is seen in the approval he gives to St. Gregory's insistence that those who aspire to contemplation must "first train in the camp of action." St.

---

[1] II-II, q. 128, a. 4, c.

Gregory, himself a monk, knew his Holy Rule: "Taught by long monastic practice and the help of many brethren" is the monk in a position to make choices. St. Benedict, while praising the life of solitary contemplation, comes down in favor of "that most valiant kind of monks, the cenobites."[2] This is in line with the action of our Lord regarding the apostolic and mixed lives: he called his disciples to himself first, and only when they had learned from him enough of the spiritual life to keep them from being overloaded in their service to souls did he send them out on their missions. To work for others according to Christ, you have had to work on yourself according to Christ. The only way to work on your own soul is to surrender to the work of grace which does it more thoroughly than you ever could. This happens during the two nights, active and passive.

Innumerable saints have experienced the reverse process, coming to contemplation by way of action. It could be argued that they were potentially contemplative all along, practicing passive prayer until God so arranged their lives as to provide a more promising environment for it. Souls who feel smothered by material anxieties and the sheer pressure of work are often lacking in courage and faith. Either because they hunger for solitude and cannot get it or because of the bad direction they are getting, such souls can linger on in their spiritual nursery when God is in fact prompting them to cut down on work and provide themselves with better opportunities for prayer. Souls would give greater glory to God, serve others better, grow holier and happier themselves if they ceased to look at the production chart and the bulletin board. What they need to look at is God—the two arms of charity working as one. *Quot ergo sunt bona praedicantium* says St. Gregory, *tot sunt ornamenta caelorum*,[3] which roughly translated becomes the less pithy "those good things which flow from preaching are the same good things which adorn the heavens."

The conclusion to be drawn from the investigation so far is that the whole matter turns on the degree of love expressed. If your activity is all love, look to it and give thanks to God. If your contemplation is all

[2] *Holy Rule*, ch. 1.
[3] Hom. 30 *In Evan.* n. 7.

love, look to it and give thanks to God. Either way you are living in Christ and praying in Christ. Whether the book says you are an active or a contemplative does not add or subtract from the work. It is grace, which is love, that is operating in you whether your activity is a burden or a joy, whether your contemplation makes for darkness or light. Christ is love, so praying in Christ is praying in love, and you are no longer an active or a contemplative but a lover. Which is why St. Gregory puts this relationship higher than any other.

As a tailpiece it should be added that theologians make a distinction between affective and *effective* charity. Your love is *af*fective when you are praying, or trying to, because the affective side of your nature is engaged in the direct search for God—you desire to love him even if you do not feel the desire in your emotions. Your love is *ef*fective when something comes in to suspend and redirect the immediate intention. The first intention remains, namely the desire to love God, but your energies are temporarily diverted. You are praying in front of the Blessed Sacrament (affective), a stranger interrupts your prayer to ask if you would witness the signing of a will, to help in the search of the priest's car key, to answer the telephone because it's long distance and in a foreign language...so you get up from your knees and go (effective).

So if charity is to be the whole virtue and not just the acts connected with it—charitable works—it must be both mystical and moral: mystical in contemplation, moral in relation to conduct—affective and effective. St. Thomas says that souls differ according to the ends they pursue: one is employed in the consideration of truth, another in working out a code of right behavior. It is to the mystical life that charity belongs affectively; to the practical life that the moral virtue of charity applies itself effectively.[4]

As an illustration would be the story of the saint (whichever one it was—St. Margaret Mary? St. Bernadette?) who was asked: "Suppose you were holding the child Jesus in your arms and you heard the front door bell, would you leave Jesus and answer the bell or would you keep on holding Jesus and ignore the ringing?" "I would take Jesus with me," was the answer.

[4]II-II, q. 181, a. 1.

CHAPTER 6
Authenticity Confirmed

IT IS IMPORTANT, particularly for the director but also for the soul, to find some sort of assurance that what is going on is truly the work of grace and not an illusion. The first area of investigation will be the charity-humility area. If in the Illuminative Way some development of charity may be noticed—actions undertaken not to be *thought* charitable but to *be* charitable—then it is safe to go on at least until a contrary sign appears which will have to be examined. "Yes," says the soul, "but I can fool myself even here. I can *imagine* I am growing in charity when all I am doing is smiling benevolently, or weeping compassionately. It may mean I am in better training for this sort of thing than I used to be—partly because I have read more and consulted spiritual people more—but how do I know that my charity has anything supernatural about it? It all seems to me purely natural: I am a pro now whereas I used to be an amateur. You don't need the Illuminative Way to change status."

By the same argument any noticeable advance in humility could be dismissed: laudable enough but natural nevertheless. But can it? Is it not a sign of humility to have misgivings all along the line? The test of possessing a virtue is twofold: do you think you have fashioned it for yourself? Do you truly believe that all virtue comes from God and that whatever you have of it has been planted in you by his grace? Those who think they can manipulate their virtue as they go along are blowing out smoke. Those who can proceed from "I can do all things" to the next words of the text "in him who strengthens me" (Phil. 4:13) are learning about the nature of virtue in general and about humility in particular. Inevitably the two virtues, charity and humility, not only work in harness but are reflections of one another. When I feel well disposed towards people and am ready to serve them, even to lay down my life for them, it is not because I am such a nice person but because it is Christ himself in me. It is he who is love, not I. It is he who works this love of his so that it expresses itself outwardly. He may do it by means of books or retreats or sermons or example, or by a pilgrimage to places such as Lourdes or Fatima, but more effectively and lastingly he does it by conducting the soul through the dark nights and the Illuminative Way.

Consequently virtue—and at its summit, charity—is not something which I see expanding towards all and gaining in muscle, but rather something which I see *by*. Such virtue as I possess, which is not mine but his, enables me to see in right perspective. It enables me to see that I am nothing and that he is all. Henceforth I am the microphone not the voice. I preach, teach, write, work, even pray "not I but Christ who lives in me."

St. Teresa tells us that there are many souls who cannot reason in the understanding.[1] Are these handicapped? Not at all. Their virtue, as understood in the above paragraph, enables them to see intuitively what others can reach only by reasoning. This must be why there are so many more simple prayerful souls than sophisticated prayerful souls. "One always walks restfully," the saint says, "when the understanding is kept in restraint."[2] For St. Teresa the two virtues which keep souls advancing along the contemplative way are love and fear. This surprises us when we expect them to be love and humility. Yet when we understand what she means by "fear" we see that it is filial fear, and so is humility and obedience.

> If we have these two things, love and fear, we shall certainly not be deceived...but come to what we are treating of now, namely the deceptions and illusions practiced against contemplatives by the devil—such souls have no little love, for had they not a great deal they would not be contemplatives, and so their love shows itself in many ways...they should walk in humility and beseech the Lord not to lead them into temptation.

[1] *Way of Perfection*, ch. 19.
[2] *Ibid.*

. . . but if they walk humbly and try to discover the truth they will not fear whatever the fantasies and illusions the devil may invent.[3]

Later in the same fortieth chapter St. Teresa says, "There are two ways in which the devil can make use of means to harm us. First, he can make those who listen to him fearful of engaging in prayer because they think they will be deceived. Secondly he can dissuade many from approaching him [on the grounds that] he will hold intimate converse with sinners." This last sentence must mean that such souls shy away from God and prayer because they see him as turning a blind eye to the sinfulness of man, and this goes against their traditional beliefs. In his omniscience he sees our sins; in his mercy he forgives them. It often happens that when people fail to grasp a doctrine they find a reason for rejecting it. In this instance—if the above interpretation is correct, which it may well not be—the objection is that God is *too* good to sinners, and lets everybody off. It must surely be the work of the devil to plant in our minds the idea that God's goodness has overreached itself, and that therefore it is not something we need take account of any more. Be this as it may, charity still remains the first mark by which the authenticity of spiritual progress can be recognized.

A purist might wonder about the commandment to love God with one's whole heart, one's whole mind, one's whole strength, *and* one's neighbor as oneself. Love for one object with the whole heart must exclude the love for another object. A cup which is wholly full of coffee leaves no room for cream. But this is to miss an important point, which is that he who loves God with his whole heart, mind, and strength finds himself loving his neighbor as himself. He does not have to make room for loving people; his love of God assures and assumes it. In fact it might be said that because he loved God more than himself he loves his neighbor more than himself. This is not an academic digression, a *lis de verbis*, it is a fact in the experience of saints and holy people. There should be nothing surprising about this when we reflect that he who said "greater love no man has than that he should lay down his life for his fellow men" (Jn. 15:13) is Love itself who is expressing himself through the medium of a human person.

[3]*Ibid.*, ch. 40.

It is significant that zeal for souls is nowhere more marked than in the Carmel and other contemplative orders. Not that all the religious in such communities are mystics or have been raised to a level of infused prayer but that their way of life and the direction of their intention elicit from their hearts an apostolic love proportionate to their love of God. Those most withdrawn from the world are those most drawn to the needs of those who are in the world. Witness St. Thérèse of Lisieux—among a thousand others.

The contemplative does not hoard his merits, does not in fact think about merits. He loves God and people, and lets the question of merit look after itself. His outward work, indeed his whole outward life, comes *ex abundantia contemplationis.* He is not an angel; he has to live in the physical world. Whatever his spiritual aspiration he experiences all the limitations of the human condition, and not the limitations only but the opportunities. "This work," says St. Thomas, "such as teaching and preaching, is more excellent than simple contemplation. For just as it is better to enlighten than merely to shine, so it is better to give to others the fruits of one's contemplation than merely to contemplate."[4] If St. Thomas seems to be pulling down the ivory tower which had housed contemplatives for centuries, it is only with the intention of building one of gold in which zeal for souls is more than furniture taken for granted.

Vatican Council II has reminded us that two thirds of the world's population have never heard of Christ, much less of Mary and the Church, and that the command to "go and baptize all people" has not been obeyed. It means that there are upwards of two thousand million souls still unbaptized. Numbers do not tell us the whole story but they do at least speak. A figure such as two thousand million shouts. In at one ear, out at the other. We not only read statistics but see whole sections of our society unevangelized. In at one eye, out at the other. Bring it into the context of personal life, of the life of charity. Is it a matter of concern to me that members of the human family are not at the same time members of God's mystical family, of his own Body— the Church? It should be because it is a matter of concern to Christ who lives in me.

[4] II-II, q. 188, a. 6, c.

Since it is in prayer that we learn to think with "the mind of Christ," a phrase used three times by St. Paul, it will chiefly be in the infused prayer of the Illuminative and Unitive Ways that the new perspectives on the charity-humility virtue will be acquired. Where the beginner directs himself towards mastering the two virtues, the proficient comes by the knowledge of the combined virtue through his closeness to God, the Holy Spirit acting directly.

The decline of joy in the world runs parallel to the decline of prayer. If prayer were part of everyday life in the world, as it was at one time, people would find joy in serving one another, even in suffering for one another. To discover the secret of a joyful life is not the best motive for entering upon the way of prayer—in fact it would prejudice the discovery—but the soul that is in the right way of prayer cannot but be a joyous person. Neither the night of sense nor the night of spirit spreads its darkness in such a way that every joyous feeling is frustrated. Our Lord spoke about "joy in heaven over one sinner doing penance" (Lk. 15:7). "I have told you this so that my own joy may be in you, and your joy be complete" (Jn. 15:11). "Your joy no man shall take from you" (Jn. 16:22). In heaven the angels rejoice over a conversion; on earth the converted share Christ's joy and it is a joy which nobody can spoil. St. Paul too is full of the need for joy: "Rejoice, again I say rejoice" (Phil. 4:4); "the fruit of the spirit is charity, joy, peace" (Gal. 5:22). Souls who truly live in the spirit are best placed to grow in these virtues because guided by the Spirit, which is love, joy and peace are no longer natural blessings but supernatural ones.

Where there is trust, the obstacles to joy are pushed out of the way. Not entirely eliminated—because joy, like peace, is something that has to be fought for—but deprived of their sting. The saints, whose trust in God affected everything they did and everything they had to suffer, lived in a constant state of joy. Not in a state of hilarity, euphoria, exhilaration—these are matters of mood, just as panic is a matter of nerves and exasperation a matter of emotional indulgence—but in a state of quiet confidence. Those fortunate enough to have met a saint, if only for a few minutes, will have been struck by one quality before all—serenity. This comes only through total response to the grace of prayer, dark nights and all, and has little to do with the applied calm of the man who has studied his face and manner in front of a looking glass.

A dictionary would give different meanings to the words joy, serenity, peace, but in the spiritual order they amount to the same thing—ready acceptance. Man lost this quality in the Garden of Eden and has never got it fully back. If he can say with St. Paul, "In whatsoever state I am, I am content therewith" (Phil. 4:11), he is far on a voyage of rediscovery; to have got this far would point to his being a soul of interior prayer. Without serenity, which goes with the integrity or completeness of our first parents before the fall, it is difficult to see how the life of prayer can be maintained. To know that God is one's sole support, one's sole and lasting security, inevitably brings about a lightness of heart which sees joy in all the works of God. Prayer has given to the soul something of the way in which God views his creation. In this perspective, man, like God, "sees that it is good" (Gen. 1:10, 22, 31).

Where the beginner feels restless, nervous, depressed when he is by himself, the more integrated proficient welcomes solitude. Solitude is now seen in relation to prayer, as the appropriate setting for the interior life. It is not an escape from people, because a serene person is serene wherever he is, nor is it a luxury any more than it is a penance. It is something to be cultivated but not, as will be seen in the chapter following, wallowed in. "The cause of man's unhappiness," wrote Pascal, "is that he does not know how to stay quietly in his room."

The curious thing about serenity, joy, peace, is not that the will can dispose of a suffering but that the tranquillity born of prayer can remain in the middle of it and survive it. To find this tranquillity in times of sorrow is a grace, and since Christ has promised to turn our mourning into joy we need never think of sorrow as having the last word. On our attitude towards joy and sorrow will our attitude towards heaven largely depend. It will show us that while we cannot in this life enjoy all that Christ came to bring, we can anticipate in faith and hope what we cannot experience in fact. We need a heaven in which our infinite desires will be satisfied, and the knowledge that this must be so is itself a joy.

Another piece of knowledge which brings joy is the knowledge that God never allows our sufferings to be more than we can bear. This is because however black the dark nights we can always say, "Not my will but yours be done." We may want him to take the chalice from us, we may ask him to take it from us, we may not see the value of it, we may think it is poisoning us, but so long as we are willing what he wills we are at rest in the part of our being which matters most. "The righteous man has nothing to fear neither in life nor in death," says Socrates, "for the gods will look after him." In the Christian context, especially in the mystical context, this is borne out not only by the martyrs who give their bodies but by the contemplatives who give their spirits.

In examining a cause for beatification and canonization the Sacred Congregation looks for the signs of balance and joy in the life of the candidate. Balance sets the seal on holiness precisely because sin unbalances. By a twofold rebellion—original sin removed sense from subjection to spirit and spirit from subjection to God—man disturbed the harmony designed for him by God. Christ's atonement brought man back to God, "at-one-ment" drawing him into union; but the psychological balance, once turned upside down, could not be put back as though nothing had happened. The nearest a soul can get back to what man originally was is by righting as far as possible the order as it had been: that is, by subjecting his senses, emotions, appetites to reason and will, and by subjecting his reason to God. This he cannot do unaided. He needs grace, and the grace to see what has to be done and also to work at what he sees comes chiefly by means of his interior prayer. Beginning in the Purgative Way with the passive night of the senses, continuing through the Illuminative Way with the passive night of the spirit, the soul is gradually being trained in spiritual childhood, dependence, integrity, neo-innocence, and of course love.

St. Teresa has some tests of her own by which a soul's prayer life can be judged right and safe. Gratitude and the sense of unworthiness show themselves as signs, followed by a willingness to suffer and a deeper appreciation of Christ's Sacred Passion. She also mentions a greater detachment from material comforts and the good things of life generally, but this point will come later when we are considering the pitfalls which lie in wait for even the proficients. Evidence of gratitude is required also by St. Thérèse of Lisieux in her definition of prayer: "A cry of thanksgiving and love uttered equally in sorrow and joy." Another soul of prayer, Helen Keller, in accounting for her "hour of meditation before God," says, "For three things do I thank God every day of my life: for the knowledge of his works, that he has set in my darkness the lamp of faith, that I have another life to look forward to." We thank God for the gift of his Son to us in the Blessed Sacrament. Do we thank him enough for the gift of his Spirit in our prayer?

Gratitude sets the seal of authenticity upon our joy as well as upon our prayer. We are not likely to be grateful for the wrong kind of joy. "Pleasure is a leaky cask anyway," says Pascal, but if we are not grateful for the right kind there is no guarantee that we shall possess it forever. This *eudaimonia,* or state of spiritual health, is not proof against neglect and infidelity, so presumably it is not proof against ingratitude either. We think of it as something which we feel and which we want to go on feeling. It would be better if we thought of if as something given by God for reasons of his own and which must be made use of in his service. We cannot begin to understand the joy of the Holy Trinity, nor even the joy of Jesus and Mary—we have never experienced these joys. But we have experienced some sort of reflection of such joys and if we find we are not being thankful for them, then there must be something lacking in our prayer.

St. Teresa's third test (sense of unworthiness) has been treated at length in an earlier chapter so we can go on to examine ourselves about our attitude towards suffering, ours and other people's, and the deeper understanding of the Passion we should be gaining. It is only logical to suppose that the more we have come to live in Christ the more we come to appreciate the mystery of his sufferings. He conveys interiorly his own attitude towards suffering and so purifies ours. It is not that we have to force ourselves to suffer rightly by studying suffering. It is rather that we come to share our sufferings with his and his with ours. Our attitude springs out of our prayer and not out of an increased textbook knowledge or sense of duty or stimulated devotion. Compassion becomes less of a sentiment and more of a participation, and accordingly becomes more of a prayer. To the extent that Christ's suffering becomes my suffering, my suffering becomes a prayer. Prayer is explicit worship, suffering is implicit. But the more explicit the suffering can become, by directing it towards the glory of God in union with Christ's Passion, the more it will teach the soul. The knowledge will come from the inside now, and not as something learned from without.

"Paul has restated the problem of pain," writes Frank Sheed, "not how to avoid it but, given that all will have their share of it, how not to waste it, how to make use of it. If we are willing to offer it to Christ for linking with his own suffering, it can be salvation-bringing."[5] In the matter of offering one's pains to Christ, the sufferer must be careful not to see himself framed in the crown of thorns. Pain is sanctifying only to the degree that it goes in the right direction and is not allowed to boomerang back to self. To be aware while suffering that this is the test, that a place on Calvary is his for the asking, that the invitation is to holiness creates in the humble soul a scorching sense of dread. What is chiefly dreaded is not more suffering but the knowledge that the suffering will be endured so badly. The sense of inadequacy seems to vitiate the whole thing. But the soul is wrong here; the burnt-offering goes on crackling at the altar because in the will it has never been recalled.

Physical pain can be charted, located, monitored, eased by the application of remedies, the sources of infection calculated. In the case of spiritual pain the whole point is that there is no certainty about anything. In physical pain you can put your finger on where it hurts. Spiritual pain pervades the whole being and cannot be explained or eased. Pain as such is not a good but an evil. God does not enjoy seeing people suffer; he did not enjoy seeing his Son suffer. In Christ's case what pleased the Father was the Son's willing sacrifice of himself. In our case what pleases him is our willingness to suffer with his Son and for his Son. In the alchemy of grace our sufferings are made Christ's and Christ's ours. If in our prayer life we have chosen Christ, we have chosen the whole Christ and this means sufferings and all. Our prayer

[5]*Christ in Eclipse,* (Sheed, Andrews and McMeel, 1978), p. 106.

life is preparing us not only for heaven but also for the cross which points out the way there.

Short of a clear call of grace, which may well come when in the Unitive Way but hardly in the Illuminative or Purgative Ways, it would be a mistake to pray for sufferings. Experience shows that when asked for and granted, the sufferings are found to be too costly. The soul has then to humble itself for the presumption and ask that the extra load be lifted. The principle of sharing Christ's burden is clear. If we are sent the cross we offer it to God and try to be grateful. If we are denied the cross we offer to God our unworthiness to suffer and ask to be made ready for it when it comes. Well, that is the theory; the practice is not so clear.

Wrongly handled, suffering tends to be separative; rightly handled, it is unitive. It can unite us with God but also with other sufferers and with people generally. From being personal it can become universal and vicarious. If self-pity diminishes and isolates, world-pity enlarges and communicates. If you were God how would you, knowing what he has said about the greatest commandment, judge a person's generosity? Not by the hours he spends on his knees or by his penitential practices, but by his willingness to suffer—and especially to suffer for other people. The holy man Job was subjected to precisely this test. It took him some time to recognize the inwardness of suffering but he got it right in the end. If Job had gone on much longer resenting his afflictions he would have sought the last refuge of the unwillingly afflicted, dragging himself through life on a broken wing. Satisfaction of a sort can be found in misery, but Job bound up his broken wing and used it for what wings are for. Only afterwards, when he looked back from happiness rediscovered, did he see what hundreds of years later would be called the dark nights of sense and spirit.

Possessing a clearer insight into the Sacred Passion, the soul in the Illuminative Way acquires a correspondingly clearer understanding of the Mass. With the best intentions in the world there are over-active, over-devout souls who love the Mass chiefly because their intentions stand a better chance of being heard when mentioned at the Consecration and during their thanksgiving after Holy Communion. They would not put it into words but such people think of the Mass not from

God's point of view but only from their own—for them the Mass is obtaining, not giving. A sacrifice yes, but the kind of act which in a mysterious way attaches merit to our attendance and intentions. This may seem a very elementary approach but it is not uncommon, and those who think in this way should be encouraged to consider what really goes on at the Mass and what it actually is. It is the painless reenactment of Calvary, offered by Christ to the Father and inviting our cooperation. It is not a mere memorial service leading up to Eucharistic reception. Nor is it a rite composed essentially for the celebration of priests and which invites the presence of lay people. In the Mass the priest is Christ, and the one "saying" the Mass is his representative. He speaks with the voice of Christ. The words of consecration are Christ speaking. In the offering and slaying which make up the sacrifice it is Christ who is the victim. The Mass is not something said or sung, it is something *done*. Moreover it is not something confined to our altars in our churches here on earth but is Christ's continuing priesthood making his continuing intercession on behalf of man. This is best brought out by Frank Sheed where he says:

> Priests and we are joining with Christ in something he is *now* doing in heaven. Calvary was complete, but we learn that Christ, at the Father's right hand, continues to intercede for us (Rom. 8:24; Heb. 7:24). There he offers himself, once slain on Calvary, now forever living, to his Father that the salvation he had won for our race should be taken and made their own by every one of the race's members. At the altar the priest, *and we with him*, offer the same Christ, sacramentally present, to the same Father for the same purpose... the priesthood of Christ breaks through to our altars at every Mass.[6]

Pious souls have been known to say, in their laudable devotion, that when they get to heaven they will miss hearing Mass. This is like missing their five-finger exercises while playing Bach, like missing cheese while eating pizza—the rubrics of the Mass will not be there, nor will the chant or the wording, but the "on-going" act of reparation will be the same and performed by the same Person, offered to the same Father. It does not require the infused graces of the Illuminative

[6]*Op. cit.*, pp. 8, 107.

or Unitive Way to arrive at this knowledge; a Catholic encyclopedia or Frank Sheed's book will supply the information. But once the theology of the subject is grasped, the light which comes with more advanced prayer enhances out of all proportion the appreciation. The eye of the spirit sees through the pages of the missal and the prayers of the ordinary take on added significance. "We pray that your angel may take this sacrifice to your altar in heaven. Then, as we receive from *this* altar the sacred body and blood of your Son, let us be filled with every grace and blessing through Christ our Lord." The two altars are seen to be one; the body and blood are seen to be one Christ; priest and victim are seen to be one Person.

But the question, as far as the frame of this book goes, is not so much theological as spiritual and ascetical. What does the theory of suffering and its relation to the Mass lead to? Forget for the moment about the three Ways and the four dark nights, and simply look squarely at the glory of God. Prayer obviously gives glory to God, and suffering potentially gives glory to God. How combine the two so that suffering becomes a prayer, and prayer gives value and destination to suffering. Since suffering and love, of which prayer is a part, are the two most inevitable elements in our human experience, it is important that we get them right and see the link between them. Indeed they are more than elements—the term suggests a static role—they are factors which to some extent mold us. So if we take our shape from these factors in our lives, allowing always that it is by God's providential will that they influence us, we must detect the difference between good suffering and bad, between selfish and unselfish love. Suffering is bad only when it embitters; then it is poison. Suffering is good when it is an agent, working positively in the service of God. Rightly ordered suffering is apostolic, is a witness, as it was in St. Paul "manifesting the odor of Christ's knowledge in every place. For we are the fragrance of Christ, alike as regards those who are saved and those who are lost. To the lost an odor that leads to death, to the saved a fragrance that leads to life" (2 Cor. 2:15-16).

There is a plant that grows high up in the Andes which, when it is bruised or its skin is pierced, sends out a delicious smell. It has no flower but serves as food for travelers who have lost their way and for the poor. Nature evidently means it to compensate for the exotic but scentless blooms growing in that rare air. The plant is called *la llaga del costado izquierdo,* the wound in Christ's side.

Ours were the sufferings he bore, our the sorrows he carried. We thought of him as someone punished, struck by God and brought low. Yet he was pierced through and brought low for our sins, crushed for our faults. On him lies the punishment that brings us peace, and through his wounds we are healed (Is. 53:4-5).

I called to my friends for help and they failed me. I looked for one who would comfort me and there was none (cf. Lam. 1:19-21).

My people, what have I done to you? When I was thirsty, you gave me vinegar to drink; and you pierced your savior's side with a lance...I opened the sea before you, but you opened my side with a spear...I raised you to the height of majesty, but you raised me high on the cross. My people what have I done to you? How have I offended you? Answer me.
(Good Friday reproaches).

CHAPTER 7
Possible Deviations

WHERE VARIATIONS IN THE SPIRITUAL LIFE are concerned, the human memory has one great defect—it forgets. It can imagine what previous states were like. It can recall details—witness Job: "Who will bring me back to the days that are gone, and the time when God was my guardian; when his lamp shone over my head, and his light was my guide in the darkness...and my children were around me?" (Job 29:2-5). But once a stage has passed, the new stage has nothing of any substance to draw upon or compare with; it has to take hold of the present and make the best of it. This inability to remember is just as well because if one were to use happy memories to force a light while in the passive dark night he would only hinder the work of grace, while if one were to remember afterwards how dark the night had been one would probably not have the courage to go on and possibly have to face another.

We are considering now the long drawn out Illuminative Way, when it is not all light and not all darkness and when memory is being trained in the "cloud of forgetting" so that it may put no obstacle in the way of arriving at a new knowledge. If, naturally speaking, memory is at its worst, supernaturally speaking it is learning to be at its best. For the state of union the preparation has to be more radical than for the other two: the state of purgation is itself preparation, the state of illumination prepares only up to a point, the state of union has to be prepared for by a mixture of infused grace and loving cooperation.

This is such a significant period in the life of the soul that the devil is more than ever active in proposing alternatives to the action of grace. The nearer the soul approaches transforming union the more subtle are the devil's attempts to prevent the culminating state. Where the temptation used to be to straightforward vanity, now it is to secret pride. Where before it was to sins of sex, now it is to the same sin disguised as innocent affection. Where before it was to vulgar ambition, now the ambition parades as zeal for souls. Where before the temptation was to luxury and material things, now it is to the more harmful luxury of spiritual satisfaction. Consequently this chapter will be a fireman's job, getting behind the smoke which hides the banked up heat and trying to prevent flames from reaching the upper floors.

After coming out of the passive night into the light of day, one of the first mistakes which souls make is to think there is nothing more to worry about, and that all they have to do is to hold on to the peace they are enjoying. If they are never to advance farther than this in the spiritual life they are content. The heights are for mystics and saints, they will tell you, the valleys are more for us. This may sound humble and safe, but in fact is a cry of defeat. Also it smacks of complacency. To add to the sense of contentment they find that their sins are tapering off and they have nothing to say in confession. Worldliness, ill temper, extravagance, gossip are no longer the trouble that they used to be. What such souls should know is that they are experiencing a temporary lull, and that God, having seen how they reacted to pain while in the passive night of sense, is now seeing how they react to peace.

There can be long periods of time when a soul may be free of inner disturbances, of tensions and temptations, but on that account to let down the defenses is to ask for trouble. Temptations have all the time in the world and are only waiting to pounce. Satan knows to the minute when to bring them into play.

There is a straight road which runs through the desert in Mexico from Merida to Chichen. After a distance of about fifty miles the road takes a sudden bend which is somewhat hidden from the motorist by a massive tree. There are accidents. During the tourist season, hidden by the leaves, vultures perch on the branches from morning to night.[1]

Twice in the psalms the soul is warned against smugness. "In my

---

[1] This is recorded with apology. The present writer cannot remember where he read it.

prosperity I have said 'nothing can shake me' " (Ps. 30:6) and " 'Nothing can move me,' says the evil man, assuring himself" (Ps. 10:6). Souls in the Illuminative Way would hardly qualify as evil men, but they can sometimes be stupid men, incautious and overconfident in being able to maintain their God-given state. The psalmist is all for confidence but allows the soul to boast of being unshakable only when the support is acknowledged to be God (Ps. 16:8).

Arising out of complacency is the belief that the ordinary safeguards to prayer are not needed any more. "I can pray wherever I am." Perhaps, but to be able to do so is still a grace, and graces have to be handled with respect. It is unlikely that you can go straight from the television into the state of infused contemplation. A batsman gets someone to bowl to him in the nets before walking out to the wicket. A violinist tries a few chords before playing his piece. A fisherman swishes his rod and makes experimental casts before settling down to catch fish. If in sport and art the specific act is preceded by a pause for limbering up, the act of prayer has to be approached prayerfully. The senses have to be withdrawn from distracting influences, the intellect has to be calmed down, the will has to be directed, the body has to be told how to behave. All this may seem elementary, and indeed it is, but it is owed to God as a good will offering, a token discipline. Not to take precautionary measures with regard to prayer is to expect either an extra grace over and above what God judges is necessary for the prayer act or to trust to luck, magic, an exaggerated idea of one's hold on contemplation.

The cavalier attitude towards the many small regulations which traditionally govern the prayerful habit is very natural when we consider the new-found freedom which the soul experiences on leaving the passive as well as the active night of sense. Less tied to a system, to a timetable, to a routine of spiritual exercises, to the suffocating worry of having to "get in" a stipulated number of prayers in the day, a number of mortifications resolved upon years ago and pledged to be continued forever, the newly contemplative tends to declare war on the cut-and-dried, the know-where-you-are. He can over-react against regimentation, throwing away the golden egg together with the goose.

There is the (true) story of a regiment stationed years ago in India which was under the command of a colonel who went strictly by the book. In fact he went beyond the book, requiring his men to sleep in the open, to add weights to their packs, to march long distances in fierce weather conditions. During a cholera epidemic he and many of his regiment died. The colonel appointed to take his place reversed his predecessor's policy, building comfortable quarters, reducing parades and marches, easing the timetable and duties, providing ample recreation. He was popular, but in the next engagement with the enemy the regiment surrendered.[2]

Under the heading of liberty of spirit any number of restraints can be thrown overboard. While flexibility is a good to be sought, it is not better than the good of contemplative prayer, which it can affect adversely and also give disedification to souls who expect a more strict control in those who are supposed to be in a higher way of prayer than they are themselves. Contemplatives can become tiresomely opinionated on the subject of flexibility, both in accounting for their own indulgences and in recommending a relaxation of discipline to others.

If the devil has got his man feeling superior to what are thought of as petty mortifications and childish pieties he goes on to suggest that the liturgy is only vocal prayer after all, and as such is inferior to the lofty exercise of contemplation. Not that souls in this part of the Illuminative Way go so far as to scorn the Divine Office but that they come to think of all external forms as being designed primarily to further interior activity. In effect structured prayer, whether vocal, meditative, or liturgical is subordinated to "the one thing necessary." What of the Rosary, the Stations of the Cross, Benediction? Be honest, you who are practicing the prayer of simplicity, how do you feel about these?

Always in examining such unfortunate by-products in the life of prayer it must be remembered that they do not disqualify but are merely deviations, natural tendencies breaking through the supernatural environment. Fallen human nature asserts itself in spite of the will to live the life of supernatural perfection. Perfection is reached

[2]Another apology. I have given this story in one of my books but I cannot trace it.

only intermittently; the soul's normal condition is that of imperfection. The failings enumerated in this chapter are given as warnings rather than as indications of a declining generosity. The fact that advanced souls can fail in these ways should not disillusion us but should rather encourage us in the belief that with all our own weaknesses we can still join them on the road they are following.

Another point to remember is that the Illuminative Way covers by far the longest stretch in the life of a contemplative soul, and that it covers minor nights and clearer days. There are no lines of demarcation which tell us where nights begin and end, where the Illuminative Way gives place to the Unitive Way—there is a lot of overlapping. There is a lot too that is learned by a process of trial and error. If the errors are chiefly considered in this chapter the enquiring reader should not let them blind him to the other side of the picture. Infused contemplation is an attenuated state, so often punctuated by what are felt to be contradictory experiences that for a soul to look for a consistent and even journey is to court confusion and disappointment.

Understandably confused, souls get tired of floundering about in deep waters and start casting about for relief of one sort or another. It is part of the perennial search for happiness, security, rest. "All men seek happiness," wrote Pascal, "there are no exceptions. Yet all men are disappointed. Again there are no exceptions. We can only conclude that we are incapable by our own efforts to attain to happiness. The infinite abyss can be filled only with an infinite object." Interior souls know this well enough, but while they are waiting to be filled with the infinite object they want to distract the pain of waiting with finite ones. Hence the need to correct dissipation—dissipation not so much in worldly pleasures, which would make them feel guilty and would only turn out to taste bitter and empty, but more a dissipation of energy. Such souls are known to plunge themselves into interests which would be harmless enough if kept under control—photography, dieting, physical exercise, sightseeing, going on pilgrimages. They are taken up with enthusiasm, but dropped after a while with the uneasy feeling of instability. But then when we cannot find what we are looking for we inevitably become restless. The interior life must not be allowed to turn us into dabblers. We can be like rich people who have everything at home but who spend their days wandering around the shops.

Manifesting themselves during these years of waiting, years of sunshine and shadow, are obsessions which, unless corrected in their beginnings, are likely to cause the kind of imbalance which overemphasizes one aspect of God's service at the expense of another. For example, a prayerful person can become so drawn to the idea of silence that he will neglect the calls of charity. He makes a fetish of solitude, and if he cannot find it to his satisfaction he feels lost. Interruptions send him into a frenzy of exasperation. He goes to great lengths to avoid people, and when he has to meet them he cuts the meetings short. Now, as we have seen, nothing is more conducive to prayer than silence and solitude, but there is an order to be observed.

Attachment to silence is on the same level as attachment to anything else. If I am attached to my silence beyond a certain point I am no better than if I am attached to material possessions. Detachment about everything is what the spiritual life should be teaching me. If I were really detached I would not mind seeing people and having to spend precious time with them. It is no excuse to say that I would be able to have longer time for prayer, reading, manual labor—spent by myself in recollection—because by failing in charity, as well as failing to recognize the will of God, I am putting my own attraction first. My values are in the wrong order. The nervous agitation which I feel before a series of interviews, and the resentment I feel after them, must show me that my desire for solitude is inordinate and needs purifying. Our Lord must have longed for solitude but his days were so filled that we are told he did not have time to eat. His longing drove him on occasion into the mountains to be alone, but this was a longing to be with his Father and not a longing to get rid of people.

If I cannot see the hand of God in the visits which so disturb me, I cannot calm my mind sufficiently for prayer. Yet it is by means of prayer, the calm prayer of "waiting upon God," that I shall grow enough in charity and the acceptance of his will to see my service of God in unity. Fragmented into different parts, now time spent in solitude, now time devoted to people, my service becomes more structured than the prayer which I am trying to simplify.

The mistake is to confuse privacy with solitude. Both are good servants but bad masters, and of the two it is privacy that is likely to be more selfish. Solitude has more glamor, privacy more luxury. A coconut is extremely private but is not the most apt symbol for solitude. Privacy has a hard shell and is covered with an unlovely pelt, but there is a curious sweetness in what it contains. With solitude as well as with privacy it is the inside that matters, and unless we can be sure that we are looking for the right thing in our pursuit of solitude and silence we may never appreciate them when they come to us from God.

People can develop obsessions about almost anything: hygiene, clothes, games, growing mushrooms, mortification, answering letters, and a hundred others. The more modern word "compulsion" does duty for an obsession except that you can have an obsession without a resulting compulsive act. In both obsessions and compulsions there is something the matter with the nerves. The complete man is not obsessive or compulsive, he is in control. He may be violent, sad, happy, exhausted, but he is normal. Our Lord was at all times in control, neither obsessive nor compulsive. Because his intellect and will were in order, his nerves and emotions were in order as well.

Even though in the spiritual life we are trying to imitate Christ, as far as possible living in him, the spiritual life is not proof against nerves. If anything there is more room for nerves in the contemplative life than in the active or mixed lives. If obsessions thrive on nerves, the contemplative has all the more reason to be on his guard.

Take the obsession with time. It assumes various forms of expression: fear that there will be no time for prayer, fear of not being in time for the duties of the day, fear that one has wasted time and must catch up by acting feverishly and thus prejudicing recollection. People can hoard time as they would hoard food, refusing to give it to other people and judging people harshly for taking up so much of their carefully cherished time. Time is too important to become an obsession. It is something not to be handed out in pennies; it should be a blank check given to God. Time, though not a physical thing, solid and palpable, is part of God's material creation—just as much a creature as a steak. Like all created goods it has to be given back to him in his own way and at his own pace. If the providence of God allows for every minute of the day, every part of a minute coming to us by his will, we miss countless opportunities by resenting intrusions upon our time. They are not intrusions but invitations; it is not our time but his. We should be grateful for the way in which he is constantly breaking into our day.

The time-obsession has a sister obsession—sleep. How shall I get to sleep without pills? If I don't sleep I won't be able to pray or work properly tomorrow. When I go to bed late I lie awake wondering if I shall oversleep. If I wake during the night and pray or read, how do I know I am not missing a chance of getting to sleep again? All this shows a want of dependence upon God's providence. If I really believed that my nights and my days were in the hands of God, I would not worry about how much sleep I was getting. If my work and my prayer are his, he must know the measure of sleep which is best for them. In the Purgative Way the problem of sleep is less pressing—it is looked upon as food is looked upon, a subject for mortification. In the Illuminative Way sleep is looked upon as silence is looked upon, namely in relation to prayer.

A more serious hang-up (if that is the expression) is the one about death. Some souls fear it excessively, others desire it excessively. Both lots lack an understanding of divine providence. Take first those whose dread of death is obsessive. They fear to think about it yet are constantly thinking about it. When the subject comes up in conversation or is preached about in a sermon they hope to find comfort from what is said but are left with greater apprehension than ever. They cannot face the subject, coming to terms with death, yet cannot get away from it. They should know that as God's providence had planned the exact moment at which they were to come into the world, the exact moment at which they will be leaving it is equally planned. This is not fatalism, it is faith. The same faith or trust must be extended to the destiny of the world, which is also a matter of dread to some. The world is not going to end when God's back is turned. The providential will which decided when the creation of the world was to take place is equally at work in deciding when the dissolution of the world is to take place. Since the grace to meet it will be given, as it will to meet our own end, why fear?

More usual, and especially in the passive dark nights, is the opposite obsession—the fierce longing to die. Unless subjected to reason and offered to God in prayer this can assume almost dementia proportions. Of all the possible abnormalities suffered by interior souls, this is the most dangerous. Frustrated at every turn, unable to find consolation either in prayer, people, direction, or books, the soul looks for relief in a wild yearning for death. Risks to life are jumped at eagerly, in some cases even suicide is attempted, in the hope that at the last minute it will be possible to make an act of contrition. Those who have gone as far as this will tell you afterwards, when in their right minds and this particular night has passed, that it was only by the power of our Lady that they came through. Mary must have a special place in her heart for would-be suicides.

For such souls the time spent in prayer is one long appeal. When any prayer, whether for death or for anything else, is made to the exclusion of praise, thanksgiving, contrition and all other petitions there can be no "waiting upon God." The intensity of the soul's prayer for death rules out the prayer of simplicity, at least for the time being, because infused grace is too delicate a gift to stand up against that kind of competition. When a petition is urgent beyond a certain point it is hardly a prayer any more, it is a distraction. "Give us this day our daily bread" is one thing, twisting God's arm for it is another. The prayer now should be "deliver us from evil," the evil of obsession and hysteria.

You would have thought that all the hazards which lie open to contemplative souls have now been accounted for. Unfortunately there are many more. Since pride is the first and the worst of sins it is the most subtle and the last to be got rid of. It comes into everything we do, and those who are in the Illuminative and Unitive Ways are the ones who see this most clearly. Interior prayer is like that slender hooked instrument which dentists use and which probes down into the roots of what is wrong, exposing the nerves to the light of day. Interior prayer brings self-deceptions into the open, showing self as it really is and making deception impossible. To change the metaphor it plucks leaf after leaf from the artichoke until there is no covering left and the heart can no longer hide. Other people can, with any luck, be deceived as to one's true identity, but I, the ego, can no longer hold secrets from myself. I am who I am in God's sight.

There is the more obvious form of pride which looks for recognition, which claims that recognition is deserved. While parading humility, pride feeds on being humble. A less obvious form of pride is shown in the amassing of head counts and excusing it as zeal for souls. Another is punctiliousness in religious observance and thinking this to be the generous love on which all will be judged. Pride gives fancy names to basic sins: ambition becomes wanting to be perfect for the love of God; desire for death becomes homesickness for God; anger becomes standing up for God's rights; romantic affection becomes the expression of the greatest of God's gifts to man. All this is pride, the covering up of human baseness which would be far less base if it were admitted. With this in mind you have only to watch a soap opera for ten minutes on television to see where the real motives lie in the interplay of human relationships. But spiritual people should not need to look to television for the truth about themselves; if they look to God they will find it eventually. "In your light," sings the psalmist, "I shall see light" (Ps. 36:9). "Lord, you yourself are my lamp, my God lights up my darkness" (Ps. 18:28). "With a great voice the Lord spoke to you from the heart of the fire, in cloud and thick darkness" (Dt. 5:22). It is the universal law of the mystical life: out of darkness comes forth light. Where the soul makes its big mistake is not waiting quietly in the dark and trying to switch on a light of its own. This will be considered in the chapter following.

CHAPTER 8
Spiritual Impatience

PRIDE, AS WE HAVE JUST SEEN, is the most serious obstacle to advancing in the ways of the spirit but overeagerness runs a close second. If pride causes souls of prayer to think they are better than other people, holier and more knowledgeable in matters connected with the interior life, greed can lead even proficients to think they know better than God. Where proud souls want others to think well of them, greedy souls want God to think well of them. So the two vices, always heavily disguised, are connected and have to be met with humility and restraint respectively. Humility teaches those who think that because they are on the mystical elevator they are superior to the common lot who are milling about in the bargain basement and that the only way to reach God is to approach him on all fours. Restraint teaches those who are impatient of delay that if they push ahead of God's timetable the delay may result in a complete stop.

There are two forms of spiritual greed, each quite different. The first manifests itself early in the sequence of stages, during the active night of sense; the second much later and during the passive night of the spirit. The earlier can be dealt with briefly, and this partly because it does not usually last long—the passive night of the senses providing nothing to be greedy about—and partly because it is not likely to do the beginner much harm—he gets over it and learns from it. The more significant and harmful form of spiritual greediness will have to be considered at greater length. As in the moral order, so in the mystical order, desire for gratification is fallen man's miserable millstone.

At his first conversion the beginner takes up prayer and fasting with enthusiasm, but lacking experience he overdoes both. He prays for several hours at a time and enjoys it. But his head is not used to this new kind of activity, nor is his body used to fasting. So weakened physically and strained mentally, the beginner does not realize how taxing the life of prayer can be. Prayer brings him delight; fasting brings him a sense of well-being, a hard thing done properly. What can there possibly be wrong in pursuing these things to the extreme? What is wrong about it is that he is substituting one lot of pleasures for another. He has renounced sensual pleasure but is delighting in spiritual pleasure. The taste of sensible devotion makes him eager for more of the same, and the fact that he feels it cannot be wrong, but on the contrary highly laudable, encourages him in his extravagance. Warning signs declare themselves, buzzing in the head after about an hour of prayer and feeling faint after undue fasting, and to ignore these is to allow an emotional appetite to rule the day. Vainglory comes into it but here we are considering the misuse of faculties, spiritual as well as physical and mental. Devotion does not always carry its own guarantee.

Just as sweetness in food can destroy the appetite for a more solid diet, so sweetness in prayer can be equally misleading. If you bring up a child on creamy cakes you will have a difficult time diverting the fare to meat and vegetables. If the beginner in the spiritual life is detached enough and humble enough to moderate his regimen so that he gets into the way of praying more quietly and in shorter periods, eating enough to maintain a working body, he will be preparing for the next step which God wants him to take. A final warning may be suggested to souls at this stage: to hide one's experiments in prayer and fasting from one's confessor, either from fear of not obtaining permission for them or from the desire not to appear holy, would be to continue one's practices under false pretences. Embarrassment, whether in feeling it oneself or causing it to another, should not be allowed to weigh.

The other greediness, which can bedevil the later nights of the Illuminative Way, is far more serious. It is, at root, impatience—an attempt to find a short cut out of the night. Fortunately not all souls are afflicted with this temptation, and they are to be congratulated because the end of their troubles will come all the sooner. Those who think they can find their way out of darkness into light will only prolong their distress and are in danger of falling into the same trap later on. This section of the book is not for those who are willing to sit quietly during the night waiting for God to appoint the hour of dawn, but is an endeavor to reach those who need to be encouraged to stop struggling. Such souls need to know what is going on and why their safety lies in total acceptance.

At the outset it must be understood that grace, neither sanctifying grace nor the specifically mystical graces, change our natures. What grace does is to show us our natures in their true light and give us the strength to do something about them, to perfect them. This is especially to the point in the matter of contemplation. Contemplation does not exist to save us the trouble of correcting our faults. Still less does it automatically remove them. A tendency in a man to see the flaws in everything and everybody is a tendency which other, less critical, people are without. Like claustrophobia, fear of heights, being allergic to cats, water divining, the critical faculty in this man is congenital. Suppose this man is granted the grace of contemplation, he does not suddenly become a miracle of tolerance and sweetness. But by his contemplation he does come to see the evil of harsh judgment and the necessity of taking a kinder and more constructive view. He comes to make allowances not only for other people but also for himself. He knows how prone he is to cynicism, and how necessary is the life of prayer to rid himself of all expressions of it.

This said, it should be clear that a man who is impatient by nature, and who finds himself stuck in a dark night of the spirit, will be impatient of the slow action of grace. He will thrash about in his discomfort and look for a way out. He knows by now enough about the spiritual life to expect ultimately the relief of light but he wants to hasten its coming. This is his natural impatience coming out, leading to spiritual greediness and even doubt about the wisdom of God in treating him in this way. Is God indifferent to his plight? If not, what are the chances of striking a light which is not God's but which might lead to him eventually? This line of reasoning, this greedy impatience, has led many promising contemplatives into spiritual and theological error. The wilderness is strewn with souls who have not been content to wait.

Nothing can please the devil more than to see souls who are well on the way to transforming union going off on a tangent and rejecting their chances of giving to God the greatest glory that is in their power to give. It is what he did himself of course, with his "I will not serve." Just as he excited the soul to near suicide in the craving for death, so now he is doing the same at a deeper spiritual level—because the soul has advanced farther by this time—by exciting a frenzied desire for light. But if the light is not to be the kind that reveals truth, what good can it do to the soul? The soul in its impatience does not look into the distinction between true and false light, true and false mysticism. It clutches at whatever light it can get, even if payment has to be made later on.

Where a worldly man who no longer finds satisfaction in his marriage turns to extramarital relationships, a spiritual man who no longer finds satisfaction in his spiritual life turns to extra-Christian mysticism. Satan sees to it that he gets, up to a point, what he wants. From Hindu and Buddhist mystics he learns new wisdoms. Instead of *the truth* he gets *truths*, instead of *the light* he gets *lights*, instead of *the way* he gets *ways*; he finds it all a relief after the darkness of the spirit. The authorities on whom he counted are exchanged for new ones. St. John of the Cross is respected as the poet of existentialism but not as a Doctor of the Church. St. Augustine and St. Teresa are diffuse compared with the lapidary conciseness of the Chinese philosophers. St. Thomas is too legalistic, St. Bernard too anthropomorphic. His spirituality becomes increasingly abstract, more in line with Molinos and the Quietists than with the orthodox teachers who advocate a reduction of images as a preparation for the prayer of simplicity. The Blessed Mother is regarded less as a mother and more as a symbol. Huxley's *Perennial Philosophy* is his gospel and *vade-mecum*.

From the study of eastern religions, the false mystic, who could have become a true one if he had not been so greedy for light, dabbles in psychic phenomena. Experience for him is the one thing necessary, and whatever heightens the experience may legitimately be used. This brings in the drugs. The particular drug may or may not be hallucinatory in its effect but if it is it stands for the overall experience of the false mystic—delusion.

There have been many near-perfect souls in the history of spirituality who have allowed themselves to be deflected after years of faithful prayer. Where laziness, sex, disobedience, worldliness have failed to do the devil's work, impatience and the itch for false mysticism have succeeded. Ambition has come into it too, because nobody is going to notice whether the soul is in the dark night or not, whereas a certain notoriety attaches to a once spiritual person who turns heretic. People will do anything to make a name for themselves, even abandon God. There is a hint of the danger of leaving God for an illusion in the words which the priest says at Mass: "Keep me faithful to your teaching and never let me be parted from you."

At the risk of being repetitious it must be insisted that it is safer to be blind and in the dark than to be seeing in the false light. When the soul sees untruth and pretends that it is truth, the devil takes the opportunity of providing personal revelations and other mystical phenomena. Such is the inquisitive mind of man that when it twists known truth to suit its fancy it wants to reach out to unknown truth which is offered from outside God's service. The devil, angelic-looking in his disguise of false light, is always waiting to fill the void left by greedy souls.

The danger of illuminism lies not only in the harm it does to the individual soul but in the harm it can do to those who had looked to that individual soul for direction. Such souls are placed in a difficult situation: if they forsake him will they not feel guilty of possibly betraying the light, and if they follow him can they be sure that his light is the true one? Elitist groups have been formed before now which aspire to, depend on, and actually experience mystical phenomena. St. John of the Cross has a lot to say about the danger of laying oneself open to mystical experiences, which he says are not to be invited and not to be looked upon as important even when proved to be genuine and from God. Where subjective reactions are given greater importance than objective truths you know that the ice is thinning. Where emotions play a more important part than beliefs you would do well to reach for your catechism.

False prophets have abounded, both within the Church and outside it, since our Lord first warned against them. We know them not by their accuracy but by their fruits. It is no good being a connoisseur in matters of the spirit unless you are obedient to the Church and orthodox tradition of spirituality. Rasputin was a mystic if ever there was one, but how was he known to be a false one? Not by his prophecies, because in fact they turned out to be true, nor by his healings because they could not be denied, but by his way of life and by his scorn for the commandments.

Though our Lord came out strongly against the misuse of supernatural powers, proving that his were not from Beelzebub, the devil did not give up. We know from the eighth chapter in Acts how widespread and popular magic was in Samaria (Acts 8:9). Simon Magus was only one among many. There was Bar-Jesus "who posed as a prophet" (Acts 13:6), and Elymas whom Paul denounced saying, "You are an imposter and a thorough-going fraud, you son of Satan and the enemy of all that is right" (Acts 13:8-10). So if this kind of thing went on in the first century of the Christian era we should not be surprised to find it going on in the twentieth. The devil's tactic is no different now. Satan deceives "if possible even the elect" (Mt. 24:24).

"This man was capable of being so completely led away by his desires," writes St. John of the Cross, "that although it is true that at the beginning he was cautious, nevertheless because he denied them not, they gradually blinded and darkened his understanding, so that in the end they succeeded in quenching that great light of wisdom which God had given him, and therefore in his old age he forsook God."[1] In a later chapter St. John of the Cross suggests that in many cases the desires which cause this blinding to the understanding are imaginary visions. "It is to the senses of the imagination and fancy that the devil habitually betakes himself with his wiles—now natural, now supernatural—for they are the door and entrance to the soul. . . the understanding must not feed upon them, neither must the soul desire them lest it should no longer be detached, free, pure, simple, without any mode or manner as is required for union."[2]

---

[1] *Ascent of Mount Carmel*, ch. 8:6.
[2] *Ibid.*, Bk. 2. ch. 16:4, 6.

There are two kinds of darkness: the one which comes from the continuing action of grace and which is purifying; the other which follows the rule of self and which blinds the soul to the scale of values, to God's will, to right reason, indeed to everything but the present urgency. This second darkness could have been avoided at the beginning if the combination of stupidity and experimentalism had been countered by trust. Trust always carries with it enough light—but only just enough—to enable the soul to know the next step. If the step turns out afterwards to have been the wrong one it is not necessarily because the soul has been unfaithful to whatever light was given but more often because the soul must learn to make greater use of trust. Mistaken steps can always be remedied by asking God for the grace to take the right ones. God answers such a prayer by taking the steps himself.

It is not their fault that some souls are less intelligent than others, but it is their fault if they use what intelligence they possess to experiment in spiritual matters that are beyond them. They are complicating the one gift which by nature they are best qualified to enjoy, namely simplicity. By not waiting until their spiritual judgment has been formed in the nights, they are applying an imperfect practical judgment to things of the spirit. A want of coordination results. "As a man raises himself to heaven," says Dionysius, "so his view of the spiritual world simplifies and his words become fewer. So too when we penetrate into the mystic darkness, not only do our words become more concise but language and thought alike fail us."[3] God is very tolerant of those who make mistakes in ignorance, even when it lands them in spiritual danger, but when they act precipitantly to see what will happen—and especially when they say they are practicing total faith—he leads them into the cloud of forgetting so that they may blunder no more. "The beneficent light shines ceaselessly on all souls: it is ever present," says Dionysius, "ever ready to give itself with divine liberality, ever ready for souls to receive it."[4]

St. Catherine of Siena speaks of the muddleheadedness of souls which has to undergo treatment, the nature of which is hidden from

[3] *Mystical Theology*, ch. 3.
[4] *Eccelsiastical Hierarchy*, III.

the person concerned. "God works in us as he wishes," she says, "so subtly and secretly that the man in whom the work is being accomplished does not himself perceive it, and if that man knew of the work he would always spoil it."[5] In the same chapter she makes our Lord speak as follows: "I wish you never to concern yourself with what I am doing, for you would inevitably rob something of it in appropriating to yourself that which does not belong to you. I shall therefore carry out the rest of my work without your knowing anything about it. *I wish to separate you from your spirit so that it should seem drowned in my depths.*"[6]

Patience, ignorance, absence of spiritual ambition—these alone ensure the disposition for further grace. If God is to build, the soul is to stand back and let him take the tools and material and go work while the soul isn't looking. The time will come when all will be explained. Not until the Unitive Way is safely entered can the soul follow the process or come to a true knowledge of God. "There is a still more perfect knowledge of God," writes Dionysius in *Divine Names,* "which is the result of a sublime ignorance and which is brought about by virtue of incomprehensible union."[7]

The contemplation of Dionysius' "divine darkness" which he keeps reiterating may dispense with the act of forming concepts of God but it never becomes so abstract that it dispenses with the thought of Christ. It remains a formally spiritual way of praying, but not so spiritual that it evaporates altogether. The Holy Spirit's action in prayer must never be thought of as ousting the presence of Christ. "Divine darkness" is valid only insofar as it reflects the action of God and works towards the love of God. Obviously the gift of grace, whether relating to contemplation or to anything else, is received in varying degrees by different people. The sun's light shines on all God's creatures but is better reflected in a lake or pane of glass than in a piece of flannel. The saint reflects it better than a sinner. Contemplation reflects it better than the singing of hymns.

When you get right down to it, man best reflects God when his

---

[5] *Dialogues,* ii, ch. 2.
[6] *Ibid.*
[7] *Ibid.,* ch. 7.

longing for union contains the least element of self-interest. Dom John Chapman says that "the *principal* stage [of contemplation] consists of this: 'O God, I want you, and I do not want anything else'—this is the *essence of pure contemplative prayer*, until the presence of God becomes vivid."[8]

It is by no means easy to eliminate the what's-in-it-for-me element in our practice of interior prayer. The "I" comes up all the time. But so long as the "I" knows its place and is content to wait upon God's action there is no great danger. It is when the "I" makes claims, forces spurious light, talks grandly about mystical experience and expertise that the grace of contemplation is withdrawn. Why should it not be? If the "I" can manage so well on its own, doing all the things for itself which God normally does for souls, why should it not be left to its own devices and get on with it? It will not get far—unless into error.

---

[8]*Spiritual Letters*, Sheed & Ward, London, p. 289.

CHAPTER 9
Contemplatives and Life

THERE ARE PEOPLE WHO THINK that contemplatives have to reduce the tempo of life and bury themselves in the desert. They are wrong. The ostrich syndrome is no part of the contemplative's experience. True, there is a renunciation of worldly distractions, but there is none of the now fashionable attitude of stop-the-world-I-want-to-get-off. The contemplative takes his place in God's creation and trusts that God's providence has put him where he is meant to be. If among people, he accepts; if in solitude, he is grateful. He does not despise the world, he loves it and suffers for it. "God so loved the world as to send his only-begotten son into the world...not to condemn the world but that through him the world might be saved" (Jn. 3:16-17). "Christ came that we might have life and have it more abundantly" (Jn. 10:10). The contemplative takes his cue from Christ. He has no quarrel with the world or with life. He knows that Christ is the *Life* as well as the *Way* and the *Truth*, so he tries to adjust himself to life at that level and live it fully to the greater glory of God. As regards the world, he is stuck with it, so all he has to do is to avoid being sucked into the wrong part of it. The principle of life is God; the principle of the world—the fallen world with its false values and philosophies, away from God—is death.

It is the contemplative who understands this confrontation and draws the right conclusions. For him it is a question of seeking the true life and living it. The false life which he sees around him he makes allowances for, prays and does penance for, tries to find ways of steering it in the right direction. As regards this last point, the contemplative sometimes makes the mistake of thinking that his vocation is to keep his mouth shut when he could be pointing the way to those who have lost it or never seen it, when he could be revealing the truth to those who are living in untruth. It is not part of the contemplative's doctrine of acceptance to lie down and sleep when there are abuses which he should be opposing. Take the case of St. Teresa, deep in the Unitive Way of mystical contemplation, who fought like a tiger for the reform of the Carmelite Order. Take St. Bernard, enjoying the highest states of mystical prayer in the Way of Union, challenging Abelard, accusing Cluny of betraying their Benedictine tradition, and putting St. William of York in his place. Where the ideal is involved, the contemplative is as vocal as any reformer—and without loss to his contemplation. St. Teresa did not leave her contemplation in order to make foundations and write books. St. Bernard did not leave his contemplation to preach and write angry letters. St. Jerome and St. Augustine did not leave their contemplation to fight heresy. For contemplatives to leave the work of the Church to apologists, theologians, propagandists, is to lay themselves open to valid criticism. Somehow they must evolve a spiritual system by which they carry their contemplation into the arena. But they must be very sure that the cause they are fighting for is God's cause and not their own, and that God is really calling them to do the fighting. This is where obedience comes in.

More immediate and less controversial is the responsibility owed by religious superiors towards their subjects, by directors towards their penitents. Their responsibility is first to follow the contemplative ideal themselves and then to impart the knowledge that it brings to others. *Contemplatio est diffusivi sui*, but it cannot spread itself if it is not there where it is most wanted. *Contemplata aliis tradere* cannot be fulfilled if the one who contemplates looks upon the grace as a private gift granted for his personal sanctification alone. So it comes to this, that contemplation has to be related to life, to one's own life and to other people's. How this relationship is to be worked out in practice is necessarily a matter for the practical judgment. The desire to work it out and the means with which to do it are jointly the subject of this book. The true contemplative echos our Lord's words: "For them do I sanctify myself" (Jn. 17:19). The false contemplative says, "For myself do I sanctify myself. . . and let them see how well I am doing it."

Before a contemplative soul can profitably work for God and for others he must try to rid himself of the first question we all ask when we are thinking of embarking upon a new life: what's in it for me? The life which we are trying to live—and we learn this more clearly in the Illuminative Way than we have learned it in the Purgative Way when we were applying human reason to the spiritual project—is above nature, is a matter of grace. If I look to its fringe benefits I am virtually tying God's hands. How can he be all to me unless, in intention anyway, I am all for him? St. John of the Cross quotes the words of Isaias: "They all love gifts and allow themselves to be carried away by rewards," (Is. 1:23) and goes on for pages and pages about the harm done to the soul by looking for benefits from what should be the pure naked, service of God in prayer. "The spiritual man, then, must restrain the first motion of his heart towards creatures, remembering the premise which we have here laid down, that there is naught wherein a man may rejoice save in the service of God, directing all things to this end, looking in them neither for his own joy nor for his consolation."[1]

Well, granted we have understood the conditions and have accepted God's terms, how do we relate the mystical with the everyday? Because it is in the everyday that our lives are unfurled, not in the states of ecstacy and mystical phenomena. When a man has come to see God's will as being more desirable than his own he soon comes, chiefly by means of his prayer but also by the right use of his intellect, to see even the details of his day as having an almost sacramental character.

There has been a transference of interest and destination. A certain abbé who was a lecturer in a French monastery was once walking in the grounds with one of the seminarians and he picked up a pebble from the ground, tossing it in his hand while he talked. When the abbé and the young man turned at the end of the path and came back, the seminarian noticed the abbé looking down as if searching for something. "What have you dropped?" he asked. The priest had not dropped anything but was looking for the hollow in the ground which showed where the pebble had been. Gravely the abbé bent down and

---

[1] *Ascent*, 20:3.

put the pebble back. "If the good God meant it to be there, I would not want to interfere with his design," said the old man. That kind of spirituality would drive most of us mad in a week, leading to scruples and multiplicity, but it shows the way in which the most indifferent everyday things can assume a sacredness when viewed in context of God's providence.

Souls in the Illuminative Way, and still more in the Unitive Way, are constantly being reminded by the insignificant how highly significant even the smallest works of creation are, how divine providence extends to all the ordinary happenings of our very ordinary life, how close God is in every waking and sleeping moment of our day. Especially is this new understanding of God's closeness seen in our prayer life.

Where up until now one was picturing Christ outside oneself, someone to be met in the Blessed Sacrament, someone to be stretched out to—"I lift up my eyes to you, Lord, to you who have your home in heaven" (Ps. 123:1)—now the attraction is more to his indwelling in the soul together with the Father and the Holy Spirit. It is now a matter of carrying God, the Holy Trinity, in the heart throughout the day. Not that one adverts to it without cessation but that the divine presence is known to be here, with and in me.

This can be illustrated by the contrasting attitudes of the beginner and the proficient towards the presence of God both in and out of prayer. A postulant in the Carthusian Order felt spiritually uncomfortable at the short space of time allowed for the thanksgiving after Mass. The monks went straight back to the cell or to meet for the Monday community walk. He had been used to twenty minutes or half an hour of private prayer after Holy Communion. It was explained to him that a true Carthusian held Christ within himself all the time, whatever he was doing, and that consequently his thanksgiving went on the whole day.

The unification of prayer and life is something which, under the action of grace, comes gradually. But it does come, and when it does it frees the soul of much self-questioning. Life is taken for granted as God's gift—the happenings of life are seen as facets of the gift rather than as independent entities. "Through Christ our Lord, you give us all these gifts," we get in the Mass, "you fill them with life and goodness, you bless them and make them holy." The service of God, life itself, is seen in unity rather than fragmented and in diversity. Where hitherto there was segmentation, now there is radiated reflection. "When ten thousand things are seen in their oneness," wrote Sen T'sen, "we are able to return them, and we ourselves with them, to their Origin, and there together we remain where we have always been."

So in the Illuminative Way the soul will have to come down from the mountain of Transfiguration to live its life in the plain, but the important part of the grace remains present. Even the winged horse Pegasus could not stay in the heavens all the time but had to touch ground from time to time when, it is presumed, he was mistaken for an ordinary horse. Very often it is not the big temptations that shatter our reserves of hope and dependence on God, but the sheer dailiness that wears us down and saps our spiritual vitality. But if boredom with the attenuated too-muchness of life is something to be reckoned with, it is only the shadow cast by the light of the sun. The essential grace at this stage is the new perspectives granted to the soul whereby the humdrum is turned into the holy.

But it is not only the unexciting that is transformed—it is to things hitherto only vaguely related to the spiritual life that are now given their rightful places in the scheme of God. Take, for instance, a man's attitude towards his friends. He is grateful to God for them but he is not tied to them as he was before. He cares for them just as much, perhaps more, but he is not planning to see them on every possible occasion. Where before there was an element of *amor proprietatis,* with its possessiveness and jealousies, now there is St. Thomas' *amor amicitiae* or, though this sounds too distant, his *amor benevolentiae.*

It may be asked how the love of friends at any stage, whether in the Purgative or Illuminative Way, can be squared with St. John of the Cross' demand for total renunciation of all that is not God. The answer must surely be, though St. John of the Cross might not agree with this, that the soul has made the renunciation in the will long ago, has offered all temporal things and his friends along with them as being the most vital to him, and God has now, with this new outpouring of grace in the Illuminative Way, given them back to him—but at a different level. There is nothing inconsistent here with the principle of detachment. You might as well argue that because Isaac was given back to him, Abraham did not make a proper sacrifice.

The principle applies to other aspects of renunciation. St. John of the Cross would be the first to agree with those writers on contemplative prayer who claim that pleasures which have to be given up at one stage may legitimately be allowed later on. Why? Because the more advanced souls no longer want them, and certainly would not go out of their way to get them. At the beginning such indulgences as watching television, reading novels, cultivating hobbies which waste time and require concentration have to be carefully controlled if not given up altogether. To the extent that they distract from the main work they hinder progress and do harm to the soul. "What is given to self," says St. John Chrysostom, "is subtracted from God." When the settled habit of contemplation has been established such diversions would not be dangerous, and might even be suitable as re-creations. A concrete instance of this may be cited. The Carthusian novice referred to earlier, when told he had no vocation, came to see his novice master before leaving and asked whether it would be all right if on returning to ordinary life, and while keeping to his routine of prayer, he were to smoke. The novice master thought for a moment or two and then said: "Yes, so long as you don't enjoy it." This seemed to the ex-novice the most idiotic statement he had ever heard. He half expected the novice master to add "and at meals you may choose the dishes you like provided you don't like them." It was only years after this that the ex-novice wondered whether the remark was as idiotic as it had sounded. Might not the explanation be that the novice master, settled in the more advanced infused prayer, was judging from his own state? From this vantage point he himself would have seen no harm in the relaxation because by that time he would not have found it particularly enjoyable.

The trouble about being in the early stages of infused prayer is that in the transit-period between the passive night of sense and the active night of the spirit the temptation to slacken the pace is extremely subtle. The pressure comes from without, working upon the uncertainties within. "You are doing too much," religiously minded friends will tell the confused soul, "at this rate you will blow the fuses and be of no use to God or man. Why not relax, pray less, eat more, get up later, play bridge or golf or fish for trout, and see a good film occasionally?" While in the Purgative Way the soul would not have dreamed of making such concessions, now the suggestion that he bend his self-denying resolutions is an appeal to humility. But then in the name of humility the lowering of almost any standard can be justified. This is a trap.

We have considered the change of attitude towards friends resulting from the grace of detachment. We can now consider the change of attitude in the opposite direction, namely towards criticism and hostility. The same principle obtains: you take it in your stride and refer it back to God who has allowed it for your greater good. You are accused of being a hypocrite; well, you know you are and would be even more hypocritical were it not for the grace of God. You are blamed for being opinionated; of course, you know you are but wish you were not and in time you may be able to correct this. You are accounted lazy, uncharitable, lacking in mortification, failing to stand up for a cause out of human respect and moral cowardice. You have admitted all this to God a hundred times, and to yourself it is matter for shame and guilt. But your prayer life, particularly in relation to the life of Chirst, tells you not to make excuses or make the least effort to defend yourself. You can feel as guilty as can be, but neither resentfulness nor counterattack may be given any rope. The mouth is shut, and you allow none of it to seep into the interior of your soul, or even into your mind and heart. Only grace can enable you to prevent such seepage, but help you it does.

This is not to suggest that the man awakened to new perspectives, seeing everyday life in due proportions, is able to amble through the rest of his time on earth in a happy-go-lucky state of indifference to human affairs; but with the calm it induces it will dispose him for the graces which God still has in store. (There is all the difference between happy apathy and grateful acceptance.) On the reverse of the coin the misfortunes which come his way are allowed for and indeed prepared for. Rather in the way that the policeman on television accounts for the hazards of detection with the phrase "all in the line of duty" or as the Empress Eugenie said as she drove back in her carriage to the palace after the assassination attempt, "C'est le metier," so the soul takes good or ill or neutral from the hands of God.

The term *infused contemplation* has been used in this study so now might be a good time to draw the distinction made between the infused graces of prayer and "ordinary" grace in the exercise of prayer. Strictly speaking there is no such thing as an "ordinary" grace any more than there is an ordinary marriage or an ordinary murder. Grace of its very nature is extraordinary, supernatural, a distinct and individual gift. However, the term is used in contrast to the "extraordinary" graces of prayer, the mystical phenomena. Such would be ecstasy, bilocation, interior locution, visions. St. John of the Cross treats of these from the twelfth to the fifteenth chapter in the third book of *The Ascent of Mount Carmel*, and explains with references from Scripture what should be the soul's conduct while receiving these favors and how to test their validity as coming from God. Less explicitly he comes back to the same subject in *The Living Flame of Love* when commenting on the third stanza: the causes of sweetness, the withdrawal of sweetness, the imperfections accompanying sweetness, the tests of sweetness, and then the greater grace of darkness.

The question is debated as to whether, when writing about the prayer of simplicity (or the prayer of simple regard), St. Teresa has in mind *ordinary* or *extraordinary* prayer. Sometimes she seems to be referring to the straightforward prayer which, with God's grace, any ordinary person can be expected to make. At other times she seems to mean the prayer of infused contemplation. It does not matter because the one would normally develop out of the other. But to get around the difficulty, not only prompted by St. Teresa but by many who have written about the transitional periods in the mystical life, spiritual writers have distinguished between *applied* and *infused* contemplation. This leaves us pretty much where we were and in any case does not matter much. However imprecise the terminology of the mystics, one thing is certain: after the initial experience of God's presence in the Illuminative Way the soul enters a very dark night indeed, and will need all the courage in the world to get through it. But until that time comes there will normally be a period such as has been described when the soul is conscious of a deepening awareness of God's purposes in creation, in human and divine love, in suffering and temptation. A telling example of this can be seen in the life of St. Francis where the point is made that before receiving the seraph's touches on Mount Alverna the saint was frequently so distressed by the thought of all the sin in the world that he was unable to pray; his anxiety robbed him of his peace of mind. After the transport his trust in God's mercy was so great that the worry left him "to be replaced by loving compassion for sinners."

"Protect us from all anxiety," we get in the Mass, "as we wait in joyful hope for the coming of our Lord Jesus Christ." Hope and trust, as well as prayer, can suffer if we are not protected from all anxiety, if we cannot be joyful in our waiting. Leaving aside our own private concerns, do we not worry too much about the state of the Church? There may be fifty things I would change (or put back) if I were pope, there may even be quite a few I would change if I were God, but the point is I must take what the Church gives me and leave God to make his own changes when he decides to.

If contemplative prayer detaches us from our worries, putting all temporal things in the context of eternity, it also gives us a new angle in our understanding of history. We see the hand of God, infinitely patient, working out his will through what appears to be labyrinthine chaos. How else account for history's catalog of cruelties, blunders, unfairness, infidelity? There must be love behind it all or he would have brought the whole thing to an end long ago. God's patience is a mystery but it is not so great a mystery as man's malice. The interior man does not judge. He prays for the world but, like Christ himself, does not condemn it. Whatever the saints thought about their contemporary world, they prayed themselves in and out of it under the guidance of the Holy Spirit. Many of them had little theology, little learning, sometimes little common sense, little wisdom of the world. They made up for these things with love.

It is because life is seen as a whole that history can be seen as a whole. When our Lord spoke about the need to have a "single eye" perhaps this could be one of its meanings. By nature we tend to split up and diversify; by grace we pull in the parts and make them one. To the saint and the mystic, who see things according to truth, simplicity and unity go together. You have St. Benedict seeing all creation in a single ball of light, Juliana of Norwich seeing "all God's works within the compass of a hazelnut," Ruysbroeck seeing heaven and earth represented in a tree. This unified vision should not surprise us when we consider God's revelation of himself and of his Church. Father, Son, Holy Spirit—one God. Church Militant, Church Suffering, Church Triumphant—one Church. Passion, Death, Resurrection—at-one-ment. Mystical Body, Sacramental Body, Heavenly Body—one Body.

We think too much in terms of parallels or categories: prayer *and* contemplation, prayer *and* liturgy, prayer *and* self-surrender. The mystic does not finish his prayer in order to do his spiritual reading or say his Office or prepare a sermon. Days for him are not departmentalized—one activity flows into another. When sitting down to his typewriter he does not have to invoke the presence of God as a man would lift the receiver before telephoning. He knows the presence of God is all about him. He lets the presence of God come up through the keys. He says grace before a meal but he knows that the presence of God is here among the dishes.

"We are living in touch with God," wrote Dom John Chapman. "Everything we come in contact with, the whole of our daily circumstances, and all our interior responses, whether pleasures or pains, are God's working. We are living in God—in God's action, as a fish in the water. There is no question of trying to *feel* that God is here, or to complain of God being far, once he has taught us that we are bathed in him, in his action, in his will."[2]

---

[2]*Spiritual Letters*, p. 289.

CHAPTER 10
Contemplative Liturgy

THE MOST LUCID PRESENTATION of the subject to be treated here is the encyclical *Mediator Dei*, so a statement from it may provide the theme of what follows. "Liturgy is the life of faith" the pronouncement runs, "begun in baptism, and finding its fullest expression in contemplation." Probably most people would assume that the liturgy comprised external acts of one sort or another, and to these the above quotation must come as a surprise. Certainly it will need explanation. The surprise comes with the words "in contemplation."

The reason why the beginning of the liturgical life is to be found in baptism—and not, for example, in ordination—is because in baptism the soul is incorporated into the life of Christ, and essentially the liturgy is Christ's act before it is man's. The encyclical says that the liturgy is "public worship offered by Christ, head and members." So according to this definition it is Christ's priesthood in action throughout the Church, paying the debt to the Father on behalf of all the members of the Mystical Body. Christ's worship is extended and renewed, catching us up into this infinitely perfect act and giving us not only a token share—"I am uniting myself with the Father and the Holy Spirit and it is *as if* you were doing it too"—but a real taking part in, a co-union.

The definition mentions "public worship" and after the reference to "contemplation" the ritualists breathe again. But Pius XII who wrote the encyclical was not a ritualist but a liturgist. He saw the subject as a whole, in the sense suggested in the foregoing chapter, and not as a matter of rubrics, ceremonial, sacred music. For him the liturgy was not a form of prayer to be imposed upon the faithful and clergy but an activity emerging out of the obedience of man to God. The sacramental system, the Mass, the psalter—these constitute Christian man's contribution to the relationship, these are the constituent elements of his liturgical service, they are his part in what the Old Testament would have called the Covenant.

Surely Pope Pius XII would not, in his use of the word "public" have excluded private worship of a liturgical kind. A priest reciting the Divine Office on his own is taking part in the liturgy. He is not performing a public act but he is certainly performing a corporate act. He is praying with the members of Christ's Mystical Body. His breviary is an instrument in the orchestra.

So where does this get us? We must realize first that the liturgy is something which Christ does in his Church and not merely something which we do in his churches. Second, that as a prayer, it is something neither higher nor lower than contemplation but, rightly exercised, *is* contemplation. In the matter of liturgical worship, misconceptions abound. So before going further into its value as regards personal spiritual progress, it would be a good thing to determine what it is not.

The liturgy is not primarily a means of creating that "atmosphere of prayer" in which contemplation may be expected to flourish. The atmosphere of prayer is not created around you, either by the liturgy or incense or the chant or ceremonies or the modulated movements of those taking part, but is something created *in* you. Where there is an atmosphere of prayer it is created by people praying. Pious societies do not bring it about; the liturgy prayed by contemplatives does. It can be argued that there is not more apostolic activity in the Church than that of liturgical contemplation. It is a witness to the glory of God at the highest level of the human makeup. It redefines the purpose of man's creation, exemplifying the catechism requirement that man is born to "know, love, and serve God in this world, and to be happy with him in the next." In contemplation man comes to know more of God than in any other activity, to love him is a consequence of his knowledge, to serve him is the logical conclusion to be drawn and a work for which grace is always given.

Moreover liturgy is not to be confused, as it easily can be, with the aesthetic appreciation of dignified worship. "I like Gregorian chant so my spirituality must obviously be liturgical." It is not a question of what you like but of what you do. Do you fall in with what the Church teaches regarding the Mass, the sacraments, the forms demanded? If you do, your aesthetic-liturgical attractions can be raised to an altogether higher level by the practice of pure contemplation.

Throughout the Church's history the true principle of the liturgy has been diverted into superficial channels. Performance has taken the place of prayer, the elaborate celebration of the Mass has taken away from its sacrificial character. With television to help in the shift of values, it is often the spectacle that people come to see and not the sacrifice that they are invited to share. When liturgical observance is geared to people's taste and not to the glory of God you get an inversion which is extremely difficult to set right. An elaborate ceremonial, carefully planned and carried out with precision, can obviously be pleasing to God. Also it can further the devotion of the faithful. But since much of genuine liturgical practice has to do with symbols there is always the danger of giving more importance to the symbol than to what the symbol symbolizes. We serve God not for the sake of symbols but for the sake of serving and loving God.

Liturgical symbols are more than heraldic devices—they are meant to reassert live issues. Rites and customs inevitably lose impact when repeated daily so there is all the more need to look at what the rites and customs represent, what underlies their required observance. In our own time the value of rites and customs have been questioned. Many of them have even been dropped. But this is a subject for controversy when what we need is contemplation. It is mentioned here because it is chiefly in contemplation that the light is given to see how controversy is to be handled. The Church will never be free of controversy and never has been—you have only to read the Acts of the Apostles to appreciate this—but unless the charity born of prayer and detachment is brought to bear upon partisanship you are left with nothing but infighting and vested interest. Even controversy can be supernaturalized if it is approached in a spirit of prayer.

Prayer without controversy is something to be aimed at by all interior souls; controversy without prayer is the last thing interior souls should get mixed up in. Bishops, pastors, religious superiors, apologists have, in virtue of their state, to involve themselves in argument. Even the most unprofessional of us may have to cross swords when it is a question of defending the truth, but for a contemplative to leave his contemplation unasked and hurl himself upon the spears is to lose what his mystical life has won for him. The service of truth is one thing; to get a name for serving truth is another.

To get back to the lessons of *Mediator Dei*, and what the liturgy is not, it is not a devotion as would be Benediction, the Rosary, the Stations of the Cross. Nor is it a movement run by extremists. In every human organization, and though the Church is divine it is made up of human beings, there is always a group which singles out one aspect of the life and develops it out of proportion to the rest. We have seen earlier how spiritual people can make a fetish of silence. They can also make a fetish of the liturgy. In fact they can become paranoid about it, justifying the exaggeration on the grounds that where the worship of God is concerned there can be no exaggeration. If the liturgy were simply a cultural expression of religion, its campaigners championing it as they would the ballet, the opera, art, it would not matter so much. Under the operation of grace they would be weaned away from a too ardent pursuit of a too natural interest. But the liturgy is more than a natural pursuit, more than a culture.

St. John of the Cross devotes two chapters to exposing inordinate manifestations of what was designed by God to be one of the primary means of spiritual development and of giving him glory. It 's commonplace to remark that a good thing which is overdone can work in reverse, and this can be very true in the case of the liturgy. Once the liturgy is equated with choreography and musical sophistication it loses its purpose. When the liturgist says to himself, "Why bother with a primrose when I can produce an orchid?" he would do well to look not only to his scale of values but to the primary purpose of his vocation. In the last analysis, what is the liturgy for? Whom does the liturgy serve? It is shaming that some of the oriental religions know the answers to these questions better than we do. Whatever it is for other faiths, and there is nothing wrong with the aesthetic taking a subordinate role in any demonstration of religion, for us the main thing must always be worship and the idea of participation in Christ's contemplative prayer.

In the way that language conveys thought, liturgy rendered contemplatively conveys exteriorly the most interior activity of man's service of God. It is significant that following the darker periods of the Church's history God has raised up saints and writers who have led the way back to pure prayer by means of liturgical prayer in its purest, and not always in its most elaborate, form. In the sixth century you have St. Benedict, St. Caesarius, St. Aurelian, and Cassiodorus writing rules for contemplatives and drawing up schemes of corporate prayer. Again in the twelfth you have St. Bernard, St. Bruno, St. Romuald and the abbots of Cluny preaching a return to the *opus Dei*. In every century exaggerations came in, giving new directions where only one was necessary, but perhaps not until our own time has the error been so openly preached that services, and particularly the sacrifice of the Mass, must be made attractive and "entertaining" for the faithful.

Another misconception to be guarded against is the view held by many that in this age of controversy and propaganda it is a waste of precious time to spend hours in the recitation of the psalms when contemplative religious would serve God and the needs of the Church more effectively by leaving their choir stalls and mounting the platform. The cry is for a new tactic, more appropriate to the modern clash of principles and ideologies. On the face of it there is no answer to this argument. But then it is not on the face of it that the essential question rests. Either you believe in the hidden power of grace or you do not. If you believe that the apostolate consists solely in talking, writing, getting about and catching the public ear, then for you the contemplative in his cell or choir stall is a drone. Our Lord did not take this latter view in his visits to Bethany, nor did the fathers of the desert, nor do the enclosed religious think so today.

Mention of the fathers of the desert brings up an interesting paradoxical point in connection with the liturgy. Primarily of course it was for the celebration of the Mass and Holy Communion that the hermits came together from their isolated huts. The Sunday Eucharist was the focus-point of their week, when also they recited psalms in common and listened to each other's conferences. Though this corporate worship, consisting of psalms and scriptural readings, was not the whole liturgy, it became what was later known as the Divine Office to be recited in its various forms by all the clergy. Such was the practice for centuries, binding under serious sin.

Today we find a different way of looking at the Divine Office. What was designed as a carefully arranged prayer to be recited in union with other members of the clergy as a means of ensuring recollection throughout the day is today so variously constructed according to different religious houses, different dioceses, different groups, that many priests, whether regular or diocesan, find they can be more recollected and more closely united to God when reciting their breviary privately. The situation is not ideal, because the Divine Office should be a community act, but if contemplative prayer is the end to which all liturgical prayer is directed then the glory of God is still essentially served. Souls who are under obedience to recite, either publicly or privately, one of the new Offices for which they feel a spiritual aversion undoubtedly gain great merit, but if their attraction is to a more traditional, longer, more contemplative Office they would be well advised to apply for an exchange to the old way. The Divine Office may have its penitential side, and should have on occasion, but it is a prayer before it is a penance.

Finally, it is to be hoped most sincerely that what has been said here has not been said in a spirit of controversy but in the hope that the contemplative and would-be contemplative may find a legitimate way of following his interior bent.

It is a mistake to look upon liturgical prayer and contemplative prayer as being two stairways running up parallel to the top floor. Better to think of them as one spiral staircase, each step and turn assisting in the ascent. Allowance has to be made for individual attractions of grace but in general it may be said that it is not a question of either-or, this-or-that, but of responding to the whole and to the opportunity of the moment. The story, probably quite untrue, of the two condemned priests reciting the Office of Lauds together each morning in their cell is to the point here. The message is brought them that in half an hour both are to be executed. "We haven't much time," says one, "oughtn't we to put our breviaries away and say some prayers?" As in the case of Martha and Mary there is not a conflict but a variation of expression. Instinctively we think of the saints as being contemplatively at home in whatever sort of prayer God was giving them at the moment—as they were contemplatively at home in whatever kind of work God was giving them at the moment. "I will bless the Lord at all times" (Ps. 34:1), says the psalmist, which surely must mean at all stages of prayer and in the different expressions of prayer. Again where he says, "Be still and see that I am God" (46:10), he is not thinking only of times when the soul has silenced words and is employed exclusively in the prayer of union. Indeed apart from those occasions when the soul's faculties are entirely suspended, as would be the case from time to time in the Unitive Way, the use of words is never entirely abandoned. Imaginations may cease, memories and associations, reasons and conceptual imagery, speculation and metaphysical inquiry will drop off, but so long as consciousness remains there is likely to be some sort of reaching out in words. God communicates himself to us in words—not always, but for the most part—so there can be nothing inferior in our communicating with him by the same means. This, together with certain actions accompanying the words, is what is meant by the liturgy.

What follows may seem very elementary but it is worth noting all the same. While the contemplative life does not consist in things performed or prayers said but in a life lived and a prayer aimed at, it is nevertheless true that it cannot exist *in vacuo*. It does not just exist. If there is a danger in the interior life of making a religion of ritualism, there is a corresponding danger of making a religion of anti-ritual. The truth is we can make a religion of almost anything, of things that take our fancy because we have read about them in the latest spiritual book or because we react violently against what a preacher has been propounding from the pulpit. For this reason the Church insists that, for contemplatives as for everyone else, we of the faithful must find out the orthodox view and stick to it.

Granted that the mystical life which is going on in any one soul is something so intimate and personal, something so unique, that the most well-intentioned spiritual director will have to act with caution and sometimes even go back on what he has advised, there is yet such a thing as objective truth. There is obedience to law. There are even checks which either verify experiences or invalidate claims. The attitude towards the liturgy is a field to be examined here. What is the soul's feeling towards Holy Communion? An attitude has grown up in recent years that because Jesus is living in the heart why receive him under the appearance of bread? If the Holy Spirit is guiding one's every movement why resort to the help of Mary and the saints? If the Father is infinitely merciful and Jesus has atoned once and for all for sin, why bother about going to confession? Granted that the Church was of divine institution, have not its official representatives, by their actions and decisions, allowed its members to form their own consciences and make up their codes of morals, set their own limits to obedience, teach their children the kind of religion that appeals to them? Thinking along lines such as these shows the false mystic's cloven hoof.

To conclude. The liturgy goes deeper than the color of the vestments, the ringing of bells at Mass, the language of the psalms, the way the sacrament of penance is administered. Ceremonial can be either the homage which tradition pays to God or which inclination pays to fashion. Liturgy itself can degenerate into antiquarianism or blossom into theatrical ostentation. It can become so overlaid by symbols that only the initiated can detect what the symbols signify. The remarkable fact about all this is that though specifically related to Christ, Christ himself is left out. True, he comes to his own at Christmas and during Holy Week, we receive him in the Eucharist, he is there in our tabernacles. But is he our life? Can we say with St. Paul, "I live, now not I but Christ lives in me" (Gal. 2:20)? Can we accept as a literal and historical fact "Jesus Christ yesterday, today and the same forever" (Heb. 13:8)? "I can do all things in him who strengthens me" (Phil. 4:13).

Mystics are not much different from the rest of us. We are all more or less like Jacob who saw a ladder in a dream but whose head went on resting on a stone. While we are here on earth it is stoniness that is our lot, even our anchorage. But the beauty of it is that God is not tied down to stones. We paint pictures on our stones, we tie colored ribbons on the rungs of our dream ladders, but is that what mysticism is for? Is that what the liturgy is meant to be? In Hebrew there is a word, *mitzvoth*, which means the direct reflection of the divine will. It is a word which we might think about in connection with both mysticism and liturgy. The Hebrews have another word, *minhag*, which covers all that is helpful to the main purpose. We might consider that word too.

CHAPTER 11
Gradual Transformation

WE HAVE COME NOW to that stage in the spiritual life where the soul is being prepared to enter the Unitive Way, and indeed enjoys touches of union, but is still very imperfect and still tossed about by conflicting desires. Some rather long quotations from St. John of the Cross will best describe this condition.

> The preparation of the soul for this union is not that it should understand or perceive or feel or imagine anything, concerning God or anything else, but that it should have purity and love—that is perfect resignation and detachment from anything for God's sake; and as there can be no perfect transformation if there be not perfect purity, and as the enlightenment, illumination and union of the soul with God will be according to the proportion of its purity in greater or less degree, yet the soul will not be perfect, as I say, if it be not wholly and perfectly clean.[1]

In the foregoing chapter we saw how there could be in even advanced souls a conflict of attraction in the matter of prayer—contemplation or liturgy. Such an opposing pull is frequently felt by those religious who have been trained in the Benedictine tradition of spirituality which takes its stand on the *opus Dei*. But it is not only in the area of prayer that the division has to be resolved but also in the areas of work, the common life, the apostolate, the use of time, the measure of correspondence and the granting of interviews. Interior souls are faced with divided loyalties all day long, and though obedience to a director or religious superior should bring peace in deciding these questions there is always the nagging sense of missing out on a

---

[1]*Ascent*, Bk. 2, ch. 5:8.

God-given opportunity. It is towards the final stages of the Illumina-tive Way, and therefore in one of the dark nights of the spirit, that the soul finds itself getting built up in trust. The anxieties as to what course to follow in the practical order become less pressing. That one is truly wanting the will of God in everything is felt to cover the alternative possibilities. As in the liturgy-contemplation alternative which finds its solution in union, so these other activities come together under the heading of doing the will of God in simplicity and trust. Always it must be remembered that this unity of outlook is a grace, and also that it is not achieved overnight.

Nor is this preliminary transformation in preparation for the state of union granted equally to all. For those of us who feel that we are never getting anywhere and that whatever choices we make are the wrong ones, St. John of the Cross is comforting here. After discussing the degrees of purity to be found in different souls he says:

> This will be understood by the following comparison. A picture is truly perfect, with many and most sublime beauties and subtle illuminations, and some of its beauties so fine and subtle that they cannot be completely realized because of their delicacy and excellence. Fewer beauties and less delicacy will be seen in this picture by one whose vision is less clear and refined; and he whose vision is somewhat more refined will be able to see in it more beauties and perfections. And if another person has a vision still more refined he will see still more perfection. And finally he who has the clearest and purest faculties will see the most beauties and perfections of all; for there is so much more to see in the picture that, however far one may attain, there will ever remain higher degrees of attainment.[2]

This quotation might almost be a commentary on our Lord's words about there being many mansions in his Father's house.

Certainly the above would account for the various ways in which certain saints and mystics have seemed to overrule accepted practice, though never transgressing obedience. Unless the vocation came clearly from God, the hermit life could be seen as a flight from the responsibilities of the apostolate. The call to chastity has been charged with holding marriage in disrepute. Fasting and abstinence are

---

[2]*Ibid.*, Bk. 2, ch. 5:9.

sneered at as marks of ostentation. "The word of God is not bound" (2 Tim. 2:9). "The Spirit blows where it pleases" (Jn. 3:8). "God is no respecter of persons" (Acts 10:34). If all holy people were conformists, the Church would indeed be dull. One likes to think of St. Athanasius sailing down the Nile and meeting his Arian enemies coming from the other direction in pursuit of him. When asked if he had seen the famous Patriarch he pointed upstream and said, "He was in a boat up there some hours ago but I doubt if you will catch him now." One likes to think of the staid St. Ignatius dancing on a table, gammy leg and all, to cheer up one of his subjects who was suffering from melancholy.

Once we have learned that the only essential contradiction is sin, we come to see something of the pattern of life. It is not just that we make allowances for sinners, that we judge the chaotic state of the world to be inevitable, that we do not expect of man more than fallen man can give, that the Church, being made up of human members, cannot be as perfect as we would wish it to be, that suffering and disappointment are part of life. What is even more important than all this is that as the grace of the interior life enters more deeply into our souls we throw all these disparate elements into the life and death of Christ. The negative becomes positive. In the alchemy of love the dross becomes gold. Without our noticing the stages, though there must be stages psychological as well as spiritual, a unity emerges where there was only diversity before.

This does not mean that the soul no longer suffers the scorching pain of guilt—it does, but the shame and guilt are placed in the infinite merits of Christ's atoning Passion. There is loneliness still, but not the loneliness which craves for companionship; it is more the loneliness which finds no satisfaction in anything or anyone less than God, and God is not to be found. This is the very stuff of the dark night of the spirit. There is fear, but not the fear of what may happen—all possible contingencies are known to be in the providential will of God—so much as the fear of wasting grace, of not loving when love was invited, of withholding help when help would have made all the difference. Doubt, the last of the four worst horrors to which fallen man is heir, is an evil now taken for granted and met head-on. It is understood to be more in the nerves than in the mind proper, than in the soul. The act of trust has become so habitual over the years that it comes to the rescue now. "I take this doubt as I would take a fever: I must apply no patent cures. I am not capable of thinking straight so the less I think at all the better. The only course open to me now is to wait until it passes." The dark night of the spirit, whatever the immediate form it takes, does in fact pass, and the less the soul struggles against it or tries to hasten the dawn, the better. The night is the time of secret enlightenment, the only means by which the transformation can be effected.

In confirmation of this yet another quotation from St. John of the Cross may be advanced. He is talking about the time of transition and illumination.

> Although it is true that a soul, according to its greater or lesser capacity, may have attained to union, yet not all do so in an equal degree for this depends upon what the Lord is pleased to grant to each...wherefore although in this life here below we find certain souls enjoying equal peace and tranquility in the state of perfection, and each one of them is satisfied, yet some of them may be many degrees higher than others. All however will be equally satisfied because the capacity of each one will be satisfied. But the soul that attains not to such a measure of purity as is in conformity with its capacity never attains true peace and satisfaction since it has not attained to the possession of that detachment and emptiness in its faculties which is required for simple union.[3]

At first sight this seems to get us back to where we were before we started to build up our desires for God's glory. The words as they stand seem to suggest that everything depends on our being completely empty. But the saint cannot mean this because his whole doctrine is that at every stage and in every trial there has to be full cooperation in the will. Where the will rejects the invitation of grace there is no enlightenment, no transformation. It must be insisted that the above quotations are taken from passages which refer to the period when the soul is on the threshold of the Unitive Way so he would naturally be more than ever reluctant to make concessions to human weakness.

Whatever the length of time it takes for these enlightenments and

---

[3]*Ibid.*, Bk. 2, ch. 5:11.

transformations to come about, and however unappreciated by the person concerned while the process is going on, there is a change afterwards which is noticeable to other people. The change may be put down to increasing age, to the result of an illness, to taking on a new job, moving into a new part of the country or a dozen other reasons, and these may be contributing factors, but the change we are thinking of here is the one occasioned by the grace which softens up the soul for the final stretch of the course. There is something called *anomie* which apparently scorns social norms. In the mystical life there is an *anomie* which does not exactly scorn but which leapfrogs the devotional and textbook categories. Conclusions are arrived at without study. Prizes aimed at for years, keys to success and satisfaction accepted as worth striving for, human relationships wistfully hoped for, recognition felt to be justified—nothing of this matters anymore. The only thing that matters is the will of God. As a beginner, one relished one's talents such as they were, one was grateful for belonging to this class and not that, one totaled up one's capabilities and calculated one's prospects, one prided oneself on having taste and being thought sophisticated. In a word, one was a person of the world. Now, under the action of grace and by no merit of one's own, one is a person of the spirit. The hazards are there, indeed even worse ones, but there is a greater trust with which to meet them. This time around it is a question of spiritual and not worldly pride. But the transformation has taken place and there is the new enlightenment to show what a fool one can be.

What all this adds up to, and indeed what is the general theme of this book, is that the soul arrives eventually, by means of the nights and the ways, at a vision of truth—the truth of God's purpose in creating the universe, the truth of conformity to God's will, the truth that exists amid the untruths of man's making. The truth is here, with us at all times, and it is the spiritual life which alone can reveal it to us. If you do not think this is particularly important then stop reading the rest of what has to be said, because from here onward the material will mainly be concerned with the way in which God unites the soul to himself in the final lap before death. The terms *Mystical Espousals* and *Mystical Nuptials* sound daunting and even embarrassing to our modern ears so they need not be mentioned again, but there is no misinterpreting the word "Union," and it is about this that we shall be chiefly concerned hereafter.

Why does God choose to introduce some and not others into the Unitive Way? How can souls prepare themselves for the grace of union? Is there a moment of initiation? Do mystical writers know what they are talking about when they pilot the course or are they drawing conclusions from their own experience? These are questions which will have to be touched upon however speculatively in subsequent chapters but in the meantime let us get down to the question of required predisposition.

Take the hypothetical case of a man who has a difficult nature but who is powerfully drawn to the ways of the spirit. He knows his faults which are many but makes no great effort to correct them because he has come to believe that they are part of him and will be with him till he dies. "You must take me as I am, Lord, and after all you have made me a weak and ungenerous person so it is not all my fault." He supposes this kind of statement to be an act of humility. In confession the list is always the same: he lies to avoid meeting people, he fiercely resents visitors, he makes excuses for being disagreeable, he wallows in self-pity. "I may not be as amiable as I would like to be but the moment I show friendliness I am taken advantage of and my prayer life goes out of the window. All I want is to be left alone to attend to God." Accordingly he arranges his life in a way that allows the service of God to come first and that as far as possible he will be left alone. Clearly there is a dichotomy here. So in order to achieve a right balance the Holy Spirit takes a hand and subjects the poor man to a series of trials. Outward trials first, inward trials next. People, impressed by his fidelity to religious practice, come to consult him on moral and spiritual subjects. He hates giving advice, which in any case he feels unqualified to give, and in addition it upsets his routine. He feels not at all drawn to serving others, apart from signing checks for them, and people bore him. More and more they bore him, yet he finds himself making efforts to be pleasant to them. He feels like a humbug answering letters of piety but cannot in conscience avoid commenting on the questions they contain. Even in times of desperation he does not think of dropping religion, which is all he has, so he forces himself to attend such gatherings of the devout to which he is invited. Though social, these meetings are convened in the name of religion; he does his best. Meanwhile he frankly resorts to escapes: the theatre, television, food, travel. Nothing satisfies. It is now that the Holy Spirit takes a hand again, but at a deeper level. Here come the dark nights. In the emotions the man protests but in the will he accepts. All that he had counted on, all that he had ever wanted, was God. And now, so far as he can judge, God is nowhere. He is left with duties and observances which are meaningless, with contacts which only show up how false he is, with a library of books which are no help whatever. He goes to Mass and Holy Communion. He goes to confession not expecting nor getting help and only to receive absolution. But it is only in this dark night of the spirit that the soul can be so purified as to allow for the grace of transforming union.

The effects of this night, assuming the soul accepts it in faith, are predictable. It refuses to consider which of the textbook stages it is in, it refuses to make plans as to what steps are now to be taken regarding prayer or anything else, it tries to remain faithful to the regimen which has served well enough for years but is not bothered if circumstances have on occasion to make this impossible. It does not look forward to an alleviation of its sufferings but finds a certain peace in having to suffer them. In actual prayer the general attitude is "I don't know what is going on but if this is according to grace and not to any laziness of mine or obstacle I am putting to it, I am content to go along with it." Outside prayer time the attitude is more definable: "I can at last recognize the drift of God's purpose in the world, and even in my own affairs there must be some sort of plan; life is just as painful as ever, and I would give anything to be out of it, but things are simpler and I find I don't so often go off on a tangent. At least the focus is God, and I am no longer preoccupied by the various means of finding God. If there is self-deception in this I ask for the light to see where I am wrong and the grace to know how to put it right."

Perhaps the most significant effect resulting from the dark night is the change of outlook regarding other people. Not necessarily, and certainly not immediately, that Christ is seen in everyone who comes along. Rather it is the knowledge, no longer accepted academically but borne in upon one's consciousness experimentally, that we are all one in Christ. Where before there had to be a deliberate mental act which said, "I must look upon this person as Christ's representative, and be nice to him whatever my feelings are," now, whether watching crowds on television or passing individuals in the street or associating with friends at a meal, or sharing a platform with men and women whose views are different from one's own, there is an awareness of what can only be called fellowship. It does not, unfortunately, always make him warm towards them—how can it if what they stand for is in opposition to the principles of the Gospel?—but at least it makes him aware of their place in the mind of God. They would not exist at all if God did not love them. *I* may not see anything loveable in them, but God does. It is through the life of prayer that I can come to see God's work as he sees it, and if he does not see with a condemning eye neither need I.

What is described here is not the result of a trick, not an acquired knack of viewing things differently from what they are. It is not forming a kindly habit of covering up people's sins. On the contrary it is learning truth from Truth himself. It is learning love from Love himself. If God so loved the world as to send his Son into it to save it, the least we can do is to try to love the world in the same way. Of our own effort we cannot do this—we see its corruption all too clearly and hate it. We see untruth all about us and can do nothing to oppose it. So God gives us with the grace of transforming union a new enlightenment, and a new perspective, by which corruption and untruth are seen in proportion, in relation to the whole. The evil is not condoned; it is faced but eclipsed by the good.

Begun in the Illuminative Way, continued and completed in the Unitive Way, the soul's vision increasingly shares God's vision until it is identified with the divine vision. Once this fact is understood there is no longer any question of "loving sinful mankind" being a fiction. It is the most important fact in the universe, occasioning the Incarnation and Redemption. It is the privilege of every member of sinful mankind to be one with this love. In the grace of transforming union the soul, while maintaining its own identity, is not just provided with a mask, a new *persona*; it is partaking of the divine nature which is all love and all truth. In every Mass we are reminded of what the work of grace opens up when the soul is ready to cooperate: "By the mystery of this water and wine may we come to share in the divinity of Christ, who humbled himself to share in our humanity." Only the Church, under the inspiration of the Holy Spirit, could claim that mere man may come to share Christ's divinity. We must know what is coming to us here. The mystery of the water and wine does not give us a share in the divine essence (or we would be fellow-gods with the three Divine Persons of the Blessed Trinity), but with Christ's divine nature. This grace, which is the prerogative of all baptized Christians, finds its culmination in the prayer of union.

St. Teresa, who was granted the prayer of divine union if anyone ever was, has far less to say about the state than St. John of the Cross. For her it was the Prayer of Quiet that she felt particularly called to teach. Of it she says:

> This is a supernatural state, and, however hard we try, we cannot reach it of ourselves, for it is a state in which the soul enters into peace, or rather in which the Lord gives it peace through his presence, as he did to that just man Simeon. In this state all the faculties of the soul are stilled. The soul, in a way which has nothing to do with the outward senses, realizes that it is now very close to God, and that, if it were but a little closer, it would become one with him by union. This is not because it sees him either with the bodily or the spiritual eyes. The just man, Simeon, saw no more than the glorious Infant. . .but the Child himself revealed to him who he was. Just so does the soul know, though less clearly, Who He is. It cannot understand how it knows him, yet it sees that it is in the kingdom (or at least is near to the King who will give it the kingdom), and it feels such reverence that it asks for nothing. It is, as it were, in a swoon, both inwardly and outwardly, so that the inward man (let me call it the "body" and then you will understand me the better) does not wish to move, but rests, like one who has almost reached the end of the journey.[4]

Later in the same chapter St. Teresa goes on, in the way that St. John of the Cross does not, to describe the soul's feelings during the prayer of union.

The body experiences the greatest delight and the soul is conscious of the

---

[4]*Way of Perfection*, ch. 31.

deepest satisfaction. So glad is it merely to find itself near the fountain that, even before it has begun to drink, it has had its fill. *There seems nothing left for it to desire.* The faculties are stilled and have no wish to move, for any movement which they make appears to hinder the soul from loving God. They are not completely lost however, since two of them, being free, can realize in whose presence they are.

As anyone who has had no experience of the prayer of union may judge, this is as clear an account of the state as may be had. Clearer, in the opinion of the present writer, than what can be found in the parallel writings of St. John of the Cross.

"It is in the will that this captivity is now experienced," St. Teresa further explains, "and if while in this state it is capable of experiencing any pain, the pain comes when it realizes that it will have to resume its liberty." For St. Teresa there is always the dread of having to let go of God's dominion and of finding oneself back in one's own autonomy. She feels that the mind and body are constantly making claims, and that these will get in the way of the unrestricted way of grace. She admits at the same time that native intelligence is well aware of this danger, so that "the mind tries to occupy itself with only one thing, and the memory has no desire to busy itself with more; they both see that this is the one thing needful and that anything else will unsettle them." Then comes a practical comment which many must have felt who have never been raised to the prayer about which St. Teresa is speaking. "Persons in this state prefer the body to remain motionless, for otherwise their peace would be destroyed. For this reason they dare not stir. Speaking is a distress to them. . . they are so close to God that they know they can make themselves understood without words. They are in the palace, near to their King."[5]

Obviously it is a mistake to compare the writings of the two saints, both Doctors of the Church, so perhaps the best plan for the readers envisaged of the present book is to have both authors on the desk at the same time, trying to see where their experiences agree. Agree they do, but it has to be remembered that St. John is writing out of his theological training while St. Teresa is writing out of her feminine but

[5] *Way of Perfection,* ch. 30, 31 *passim.*

entirely orthodox personal experience. The advantage of St. John is that he can be looked up; he is the professional who splits up his subjects neatly under headings and is precise in his use of words. That he is a poet as well makes him extremely readable. St. Teresa is that rare mixture, the gifted amateur who writes out of her experience which is at once unique and helpful to all interior souls. She does not seem to trouble about style, yet it is her haphazard style which makes her works on the subtleties of the spiritual life so popular in every age.

Before leaving St. Teresa for a contemporary author who treats of the same stage of advanced prayer, attention should be drawn in the above quoted passage to the desire to remain motionless while praying and the fear that to stir will only cause distress and distraction. Earlier in the Illuminative Way souls sometimes felt attracted to walk about slowly out of doors or in a cloister (if only to keep awake), but now in the prayer of quiet all idea of movement is repugnant to them. If someone tries to attract their attention by touching them, however lightly, it is almost a physical pain. We are not talking here of the state of ecstacy, when the body is rigid and insensible to touch, but simply of the early mystical prayer of quiet which has developed out of the prayer of simple regard. With infused contemplation, as distinct from what many would like to call *applied* contemplation, the soul once settled in a suitable bodily posture wants to stay in the same position until the time is over, and when the time of prayer is over there is a marked reluctance for quick action.

Where it is a question of reciting the Divine Office privately or saying the Rosary the soul feels correspondingly drawn to a slower pace and a more retired locality for the exercise. In the Purgative and earlier Illuminative Ways most souls instinctively wanted to make the most of those times when attention came easily to race ahead in concentrated effort before distractions should come along again and spoil it all. Souls tend to behave differently now, lingering recollectedly over the words whether distractions are present or not. Distractions anyway are not the worry that they were before; they may be just as frequent but the soul takes them in its stride and rises above them. They are referred to God with suitable apology along with the prayers that are being said. All vocal prayers, whether read from the missal or the breviary, are as though sent out to God through a transparent page. The beads of the Rosary are as it were "cat's-eyes" strung along the darkened road.[6]

Reference should be made in this chapter to a recently published work which bears out much of what has been said here of the various darknesses which precede the grace of transforming union and the settled state of the Unitive Way. The book is all too short and is called *The Turning Road* by Ralph Kibildis.[7] It is to be recommended particularly for Part II, "Under the Juniper Tree" which gives a dialogue between God and the soul. These thirty or so pages describe as faithfully, and more intimately, as anything that has been written today the trials endured by the soul in the passive nights. The account is all the more remarkable because the writer, who is now dead, was not a student of the spiritual classics. His writings, which were not written for publication, should be particularly helpful to those who are attracted to the interior life but are put off by the vast amount of literature which they imagine will have to be covered before they can safely get anywhere along the way. Kibildis will show that surrender and trust are what are needed, and that the Holy Spirit will show them what to do next. But it will be in the dark that this enlightenment will come. In parenthesis the Kibildis book is subtitled *One Man's Spiritual Journey*. That is what he evidently thought when he wrote the book, but those who read it, even those looking back from the Way of Union, will recognize the signs of a pretty general experience. In whatever stage we happen to be, it is always a relief to come across something which is genuine, accurate, and free of fancy and guesswork.

---

[6]In case "cat's-eyes" are used only in England, they are reflectors set into the white line at intervals of ten to twenty yards showing motorists at night, by the light of their headlights, where their side of the road lies.

[7]Living Flame Press, Locust Valley, NY, 1981.

CHAPTER 12
Just Keeping On

OF ALL THE STAGES in the spiritual life we have come now to that which
is the most puzzling, the most unexciting and, in some way, the most
important. Puzzling because one does not know where one is or how to
find signs of verification; unexciting because life appears to be entirely
without interest, natural or supernatural; important because even at
this point, before final mystical union is brought about, it is possible to
go back on the whole thing. "It is simply not worth it," the soul can say,
"I have suffered enough and where has it got me? If I go on with it I
may have to suffer more, and how do I know at the end of it that the
whole thing has not been a delusion?" Ultimately the test is always the
test of faith. Trust or give up. An enclosed nun, far advanced in
contemplative prayer, once said to the present writer: "It is like
clinging on to the the side of a house by the paint, and the awful part is
that one doesn't mind if one slips. I don't want to climb back again but I
know in my heart I must."

Interest in the aesthetic side of the liturgy has long since petered
out; even Christmas and Easter now arouse memories rather than
devotion. Natural beauty arouses real but momentary appreciation;
one salutes it, refers it to the glory of God, and instantly forgets it.
There is a certain pleasure in food and drink but not enough to cause
meals to be looked forward to, and even when they have been enjoyed
the ensuing sense of guilt makes the enjoyment not worthwhile. There
is no delight in company any more, and when someone comes along to
whom one is deeply attracted one suspects one's motives too much to
follow up the relationship. So what is left? Art? The intellectual life?

Achievement? These things are valued readily enough, but as though seen through a thick plate of glass. They don't mean anything to *me*. As far as communication goes they are like the man in the television studio who is making signs, holding up boards, drinking his cup of coffee, but who cannot be heard, liked or disliked, because he is on the other side of the glass and is not interested in me anyway as a person, only as a performer. Life goes on because I cannot stop it, but I have no liking for it. Is this the last of the dark nights? Presumably it must be. At least it is the setting for the essential darkness which is the conviction that one has lost God.

At this stage in the soul's pilgrimage the works of the mystics may seem to be too forbidding. St. John of the Cross goes on and on about emptiness and the renunciation of all natural desire. The author of the *Cloud* warns constantly against "sensible comforts." Dionysius is hardly more encouraging. Nevertheless it is to St. John of the Cross that we need, in this last run of the course, to refer. For clear-cut directives there is no writer to equal him. For encouragement to persevere, the works of St. Teresa, Walter Hilton, Ruysbroeck, Richard Rolle, Père de Caussade and Dom John Chapman make easier reading. Thomas Merton, particularly in his earlier writings, can hardly be improved upon. While the style of the *Cloud*, the unusual expressions of Richard Rolle, or the metaphysical investigations of Dame Julian of Norwich may seem flamboyant to modern ears, the doctrines put forward by these authors are as orthodox as those of St. John of the Cross.

In view of what has just been said, the author of the *Cloud of Unknowing* says pertinently: "Hereby mayest thou see that we should direct all our beholding to this meek stirring of love in our will...for all other sweetness and comfort, bodily or ghostly, be they never so pleasing or so ghostly we should maintain a manner of heedlessness toward them. If they come, welcome them, but lean not too much on them for fear of feebleness."[1] So much for the time of preparation; now for the introduction into the state of union which is described in the later work, *The Epistle of Privy Counsel*. "In great commendation

[1]Ch. 50.

of this sweet subtle working, the which in itself is the high wisdom of the Godhead graciously descending into man's soul, *knitting and oneing it unto himself in ghostly prudence of spirit*...he is a blissful man that may find this oneing wisdom and that may abound in his ghostly working in the offering up of his own blind feeling of his own being, all curious knowledge of learning and of nature put far back."[2] This is one of the best descriptions of the grace of transforming union to be found. Other authorities, notably Dionysius, Tauler, Garrigou-Lagrange and many others explain what it *means* but few describe how it *happens*.

Reading between the lines one may judge that the author of the *Cloud* came up against some troublesome directors who wanted to keep him to meditative exercises when his whole attraction was to a more interior and simpler prayer. Confessors today, feeling out of their depths at the mere mention of contemplation, are fortunately more ready to allow souls a greater freedom in the ways of the spirit. It is interesting to find that Father Augustine Baker, commenting on the *Cloud*, compares the author's use of the words *understanding, reason,* and *will* with the tendency among other writers to give undue importance to *memory, imagination,* and *devotion*. He shows also how much the *Cloud* has borrowed, with acknowledgment, from the writings of Dionysius, especially in this particular subject. "Do thou, Timothy, leave the senses and sensible exercises, and all sensible and intelligible things, keeping them under or suppressing them with a strong endeavor of the mind (and this is the *cloud of forgetting*), and rise up (this is *consurrection* or *elevation*) unknowingly (this is the *cloud of unknowing* or the darkness of faith) to union with God, who is above all substance and knowledge."[3]

At this point, after so much talk about suppressing "all sensible and intelligible things," the reader might justly ask, "How does this affect the soul's ordinary day? I can see that while praying there should be 'a strong endeavor of the mind' to smother memory, imagination and emotion, but from these mystical authorities there is at least the

---

[2] *The Epistle of Privy Counsel*, ch. 5.
[3] *Mystical Theology*, ch. 1.

implication that all the powers of the mind are to get lost in the cloud of unknowing. Does this darkness of faith which they all insist on, in practice reduce a man's ordinary life to that of a vegetable?" Such an objection is not as absurd as might be thought. When someone is referred to as a "mystic" there is commonly the assumption that here is a person who wafts through his day in a state of bemused abstraction, unconcerned with the affairs of men and holding intellectual, cultural, and practical matters in scorn. Bodily pleasures, it goes without saying, are well outside the mystic's ambience. Do people in this advanced state of spirituality which Dionysius, the author of the *Cloud*, Father Baker and others are considering, behave normally or would they be singled out at once as being peculiar? Do they go to parties, play the piano, read the paper, take sides in politics?

By way of answer it would be impossible to generalize here. Souls in the Unitive Way would probably not want to take the initiative where the social life is concerned, but nor would they risk offending people by never accepting an invitation. They would choose to live in low key, avoiding worldly association as far as possible, but not making themselves conspicuous by doing so. If their interests were cultural before they were granted the grace of transforming union the same interests would survive after it—but with a difference. (The difference would be that they would be able to drop the particular interest at a moment's notice without the least resentment and, if occasion demanded, take it up again without the least distraction.) As to current affairs, where the good of souls were at issue, there might be the obligation to vote but there would certainly not be any meddling or demonstrating. Irresponsibility or laziness would not come into this; it would simply be a question of leaving secular issues in God's hands. In short it should not be imagined, in spite of what can be quoted from the mystics in a way which might mislead, that souls in even the highest reaches of prayer have washed their hands of everything to do with contemporary civilization. On the contrary they know themselves to be all the more deeply involved in their time because God has placed them in this time and in no other because he has given them a particular mission to fulfill. The fulfillment has to be in his way, which has now in the process of contemplation become theirs, and not according to the generally accepted meaning of a "mission." They render to God what is God's, to Caesar what is his.

St. Nicolas of Flue, after nineteen years as a hermit during which his only food was the Eucharist, was summoned to Stans by rival delegates to advise on how to prevent civil war in Switzerland. After working through the night he came up with a proposal which all could agree upon and the war was averted. The contemplation of Blessed Herman the Cripple did not prevent him from becoming a master of arithmetic, geometry, astronomy, history, poetry, music. He produced the first medieval chronicle and composed some of the Church's finest hymns (including the *Alma Redemptoris Mater*). Examples of this kind are endless and, if further evidence is needed, there are the works produced when such favored souls of God were dead—witness the influence of St. Thérèse of Lisieux which derived from the life of union which she led within the enclosure of her Carmel. In our own time consider what has been achieved by such souls of prayer as Padre Pio and Mother Teresa of Calcutta. When God wants it to, the hidden life of union with him can burst out in the most astonishing way. "All the life of a good Christian soul," wrote St. Augustine, "is nothing else but only a holy desire," and when he crowns this desire in the Way of Union there is nothing that the good Christian soul cannot do. Why? Because it will be God working through him without the least hint of opposition.

In view of what has been said in this chapter about the amount which souls in the Unitive Way can accomplish without loss to their union, a word of caution might be added. In the first place such souls are the exception. In the second place it is because God has called them to do these kinds of works that their work is fruitful. If souls in the way of union were to take up a particular activity because they thought they might be good at it, their prayer would drop to a lower level, and even though they might persuade themselves that they were undertaking the work for the greater glory of God, the work itself would be of no great value. This is not a question involving sin; it is a question of evading an appropriate grace.

The persuasion to make this mistake, or, if you like, this infidelity to grace, is pressing and comes generally in one of two forms, and sometimes in both together. The first could be expressed by the soul saying, "I have reached a point now in the spiritual life where God seems to have deserted me and where I am doing no good either to myself or to other people. At least if I go to work on the corporal and spiritual works of mercy I shall be guaranteeing my salvation whereas if I go on as I am I shall probably sink lower and lower into despair. At the judgment God cannot condemn me for working for souls whereas he could quite well condemn me for not working for anybody, even for myself, and despairing." The second persuasion is less complex: "I am lonely beyond all bearing, and unless I get out and meet people—trying to help them of course—I shall go mad." As will be seen at once the whole trouble arises from lack of trust.

Leaving aside those who are sidetracked into the reassuring world of being active, there are the far more numerous souls who are content to wait upon the providence of God and cut no ice in the world whatever. Their mystical life does not show. They live their lives as they find it, in the circumstances of their ordinary vocation. No frills. They get up in the morning, wash, dress, make their morning offering as they have done since they were children, and go to work. They remain more or less in God's presence throughout the day, and at times very intimately in God's presence, but they do not make any dodges or mental contrivances to achieve this, knowing that if they did they would be involved in multiplicity and become slaves to a machine.

Union with God is no longer something hedged in. It has become so freed from the textbook system that without conscious checking up it fulfills all systems and goes beyond them. For such souls spirituality and everyday life are synonymous, unified not as the result of personal industry but by the work of grace. As regards responsibility towards others, and the life of fraternal charity in general, the soul does not have to rack its memory—as it would in the case of the soul who has left the unitive life in the name of service to others—for experiences and lessons which could be helpfully passed on. Where help is required, the soul assumes that the Holy Spirit will be there to say what should be said.

Instinctively the soul knows that by making a grab at mystical knowledge and experience it will be left empty-handed. Greediness, too much conceptualism, assumption of mystical superiority, will spoil the whole thing. Someone has said: "Brush your clothes, wash your dishes, answer your letters, don't keep people waiting, and if you are in the state of spirituality where God wants you to be you can't go wrong." This may be an oversimplification but it is a comfort to know that when someone asked the Chinese philosopher Pai-chang, "I have been seeking for Reality all my life but do not know how to go on with my search," the answer he was given was, "It is very much like looking for an ox when you are riding one." The search is being conducted in what Dionysius called the "luminous darkness."

So it may be deduced that the vast majority of souls whom we are considering feel drawn to, and in fact are given the opportunity to, live withdrawn uneventful lives. They live normal working lives but are not conspicuous for apostolic enterprise. When they mention this lack, with a sense of guilt, to their confessor they are in danger of being saddled with parish breakfasts, fund-raising events, school outings. All too many confessors have preconceived ideas about the ways of mysticism which make them say, "Drop St. John of the Cross and read what I have written in this week's parish bulletin." Such priests belong to the school of "I'm okay and you are okay—or would be if you came off your mystical high horse—so don't come to confession again until you have something worthwhile to confess." This is not meant to be an attack on the hardworked clergy so much as a suggestion that priests are often in more need of direction and assistance than their penitents.

The example of contemplative souls living in the world will not escape notice, and their advice will be sought. When controversial issues relating to the Church come up they can be counted upon to present, humbly and without partisan prejudice, the more spiritual, perhaps the more doctrinal, aspects of the case. They do not want to argue but it may be necessary to give their opinion. Certainly they would not, out of human respect or moral cowardice, keep silent. This is only what you would expect of one whose mind is habitually united with Christ's. Such a soul may say during the argument, "Well, this is what I think," but in virtue of their unitive life, of their participation with the mind of Christ, they are saying what Christ thinks.

In justification of the above, we have Fr. Baker commenting on the fifty-second to the fifty-fourth chapters of the *Cloud*:

> Here the author treateth of the honest, plain, simple and secure lives of mystical men, both interiorly before God and exteriorly before men, of those who proceed by the will. They are free from all solicitude about their external behavior in words or in deeds; they seek to please not men but God; they desire not to be esteemed by others or honored, but walk as it were with an open heart, free from all dissimulation and false meaning. And on the other hand our author showeth the false, perilous, subtle and hypocritical behavior of those who walk by the exercise of their wits. These are solicitous to please men and to be esteemed by them, and yet in the end they are cheated in their hope. For they must needs come to be discovered and known for what they are.[4]

There are certain signs, none of them completely satisfying, which are designed to show how true or false we are in our service of God in contemplation. If they were perfectly satisfying the life would not be that of faith, which is the one essential necessity from start to finish. Before these will be dealt with (in a later chapter) it may be a help to the reader's peace of mind to know how differently God leads different souls. When in the depths of despair, for which a soul may find no precedent in the experience of other souls, there must always be that apparently thinning shred of trust which holds on to the belief that God knows what he is about and that even in this particular blankness there must be some solution which will appear before the end—or after the end.

Of all the classical spiritual writers St. John of the Cross is the most meticulous about the progressions from one state to another, from one darkness to another, from the Purgative to the Illuminative to the Unitive Ways. Yet even he admits that there are degrees of graces granted to different souls and they graduate from "beginners" to "proficients" to "the perfect." Since we are mostly concerned with beginners and proficients, let the perfect pick up what they can from the ensuing chapters.

[4]*Commentary*, p. 209.

What have we got so far? A beginner who wants to serve God in full perfection. He offers all he has got—body, heart, spirituality such as he conceives it to be, hopes for the future, willingness to embrace the cross—and his offer is accepted. When grace has got to work on the offering and flattened out the soul, the process of spiritually building up begins. This means a transfer from feeling to faith, from the natural to the supernatural. You would think that this would be the end of it, that there would be nothing more to be done. But transformation goes deeper than this—it involves identification. For identification there has to be more than the desire to relive the life of Christ in the setting of one's own life. It means actually reliving it. There is a difference between the soul being united in will and being unified in grace.

As may readily be appreciated there will be degrees in such a development. "After the same manner," says St. John of the Cross, "we may describe the condition of the soul with relation to God in this enlightenment or transformation. For although it is true that a soul, according to his greater or lesser capacity, may have attained to union, yet not all do so in an equal degree, for this depends upon what the Lord is pleased to grant to each one. It is in this way that souls see God in heaven: some more, some less. But all see him and all are content for their capacity is satisfied."[5] This is in line with the *Cloud*, which, after a long account of the way in which God calls souls to *ordinary* ways of prayer (meditation, discursive prayer, immediate acts and aspirations) the treatise goes on to speak of *extraordinary ways*: "That by which he calleth some special souls, as he did St. Catherine of Siena and St. Teresa and divers others, especially of the sex of women, with whom he *did not hold the ordinary course that he holds with others*, but called them to divers graces and favors *when they had little or nothing disposed themselves for the deserving or receiving of the same.*" And again he makes the same point later on: "God did not keep them to the ordinary and usual course that he holdeth with others whom he guideth as it were by a more certain and set way without any great varying. . . whereas the course he holds with these special souls were

---

[5] *Ascent*, Bk. 2, ch. 5:10.

not only different from those of ordinary good souls but also from one another's courses."[6]

St. John of the Cross arrives at the same conclusion but from the other side: he puts down the inequality of treatment at God's hands to the inadequacy of the soul. "The soul that attains not to such a measure of purity as is in conformity with its capacity never attains to true peace and satisfaction since it has not attained to the possession of that detachment and emptiness in its faculties which is required for simple union."[7]

These passages from the *Cloud* and the *Ascent* have been quoted with the idea of correcting the belief that God pledges himself to a uniform system involving a particular sequence, an ordered progression, and idiom of its own in which ordinary words are given unusual meanings. This makes the spiritual life into an obstacle race with a starting pistol, a finishing tape, little flags along the course which tell you how far you have still to go and marks taken off for bungling the obstacles. This is not to say that God indulges in favoritism or makes his rules as he goes along. All are favorites, and there are only two rules which he judges by, namely trust and love. Where he finds trust and love he forgets about the labels and lifts the lines of demarcation. Can you imagine the Curé of Ars worrying about whether he was in the active or passive night of the spirit or Don Bosco preparing his boys for the knowledge of sublime nothingness? Had the twelve apostles to graduate from the Purgative to the Illuminative Way before they qualified for the unitive life with Christ? (Garrigou-Lagrange thinks the apostles had to go through the stages, but his argument, on the basis of the illustrations he gives seems farfetched.)

There is a spiritual author who writes of the states we have been reviewing and who has never seemed to have enjoyed the popularity he deserves. This is Richard Rolle of Hampole, who was writing in England somewhere about the middle of the fourteenth century (and therefore would have been roughly a contemporary of the author of the *Cloud*, Juliana of Norwich, Walter Hilton in his own country and

---

[6]*Cloud*, Baker's *Commentary*, ch. 3.
[7]*Ascent*, Bk. 2, ch. 5.

of John Tauler, Henry Suso, John Ruysbroeck and Catherine of Siena on the continent). Perhaps it is his lyrical style which has caused readers to think of him as superficial and mannered, or perhaps it is his eccentricity of life which made him suspect as a serious writer of pure mysticism. Love was his almost exclusive and obsessive theme, and he sang of so many facets of it that one's attention is inclined to wander. In his general conduct he was so far from being a conformist that in the parish to which he belonged he was virtually ostracized and sometimes even turned away from Mass. The parish priest can hardly be blamed for not restraining his flock from closing the church doors against a parishioner who would arrive in his sister's dressing gown and then take his place on a back bench from which he would rise when the rest knelt, sitting when the rest stood and kneeling when it pleased him.

With the intention of bringing out a scholarly edition of Rolle's works to be prefaced by an account of his life, Mgr. Robert Hugh Benson studied the available material for years but was told by a publisher that there would be no market for Rolleana. So instead Benson used much of what he had collected in writing a biographical novel which he called *Richard Raynal, Solitary* which was an excellent book but which did little to revive interest in so singular a character or so solid a body of mystical writing.

CHAPTER 13
An Attempt at Clarification

THE SIMPLEST WAY IN WHICH to put the material to be dealt with in this chapter would be to draw a diagram. But since there is nothing which so daunts us in learning about God's handling of the soul as lines and figures, the use of paragraphs should seem less cold and scientific. In the foregoing pages we saw that the spiritual life is not governed by the formulae given to it by the authorities. Nevertheless it can be helpful to learn from the experience of these authorities how the working of grace normally proceeds. With some such plan in our minds, always allowing for the flexibility already discussed, we should be able to find reassurance from an accepted procedure where the inward assurance is lacking. From this somewhat lifeless study we can go back to seeing how the mystical life reacts within the framework. Much of what immediately follows has been touched upon earlier, so here we are putting into categories the findings of personal experience.

First there is the way of beginners, the Purgative Way, which is characterized by conversion from sin and the more obvious forms of worldliness. Prayer at this stage is composed of devotional practices, vocal prayers, meditation on the scriptures and the feasts and doctrines of the Church. Self-denial is practiced, works of charity are undertaken. Early in the Purgative Way, the exercise of meditation is felt to be a mental gymnastic and not a prayer. Then comes the first period of transition when the soul is drawn through the prayer of forced acts, repeated phrases, spontaneous affections, to an increasingly simplified activity which is the beginning of what many would call "applied contemplation" but which is better described—because it is now more the work of grace than the work of mental industry—as the prayer of simple regard. How far the "active night of the senses" is still at work here would vary according to the docility or stubbornness of the particular soul, but with the early experience of infused prayer the Illuminative Way may be said to have begun. With it comes the second night, the passive purgation of the senses—the interior senses this time.

By this time the beginner has become, though he does not feel he has become, the proficient. For most souls this is a time of many ups and downs, of deep uncertainty, and of longest duration. For one thing the guidelines which encouraged the soul to move on from meditation to the prayer of simple regard (these guidelines are mentioned at great length by St. John of the Cross in his thirteenth, fourteenth, and fifteenth chapters of the *Ascent*) have by now done their work and give no instructions as to another possible transition. For another thing the passive nights are far more painful and searching than anything experienced in the passive night of sense. The degree of infused contemplation enjoyed during the Illuminative Way will again, to a large extent, depend upon the generosity of the individual soul. To rebel against the nights of the spirit is to delay the soul's purification and limit the degree of illumination. This is not the place to go into it but for a general knowledge of the subject it is now, when the Illuminative Way is about to give place to the Unitive Way, that visions, revelations, locutions and other mystical phenomena declare themselves. Later, when the Unitive Way becomes the soul's settled state, the phenomena tend to decrease and even cease altogether. It should be noted however that according to Père Garrigou-Lagrange, souls at the highest level of the Unitive Way are granted intermittent visions of the Blessed Trinity. It is in the unitive life, according to this author, that the last remnants of spiritual pride disappear. When you consider what the soul has to go through in the way of humiliation to get to that stage this does not surprise us.

Now that the soul is either on the verge of the Unitive Way or in its early stages we can examine some of the features regarding it. In this we are handicapped because different authorities give us different accounts not only of how the state is reached but of its permanence. Is the initiation sudden as it was in the case of St. Francis and St. Teresa, or does the soul come to a gradual awareness of a state quite other from what was enjoyed in the Illuminative Way? And again, once established in the state of union is it possible to let go by infidelity and start dropping down the ladder by which it came up? Since the Church has not pronounced upon these points, we are free to form our own opinions. As to the first it would seem reasonable to believe that the dramatic introduction is the exception: there must be countless souls who, without formulating the fact, and even perhaps without fully understanding it, are in the closest union with God to be found on earth. They have never seen the diagrams, never studied the tables, they have never read the textbooks, all they know is that they love God above all else and that they love all else in him. They do not care what happens to them because they trust. If authority steps in and tells them they are deluded they accept the obedience without argument but there is nothing they can do to change the love that is within them. God sees to that. This is not at all the same as when authority tells heretics they are wrong. The heretic insists he is right and defies obedience. The mystic respects obedience, makes no claim that he is right and authority is wrong; it is simply that God with whom he is united keeps his mystical union alive as before.

In regard to the second point, namely whether the soul once in the way of total union can slip back, it is possible that more has been read into the term "nuptial union" than should be. The indissolubility of human marriage may have given rise to the idea that in the mystical union between the soul and God there can be no desertion, no separation. This would be the view taken by St. John of the Cross who speaks of union "once and for all," a state in which "the innocence of Adam is restored," a state "wholly spiritual," yet one which is "not to be observed by the devil." St. John admits that the devil can still "produce a certain horror and perturbation of spirit which at times is most distressing to the soul."[1] In *The Dark Night of the Soul* further light is shed on St. John's thinking as regards the permanence of the state of union. "The tenth and last step of this secret ladder of love causes the

---

[1] *Spiritual Canticle*, stan. 14, 22, 23, and *Dark Night*, Bk. 2, ch. 23.

soul to be wholly assimilated to God by reason of the clear and immediate vision of God which it then possesses."[2] In *The Spiritual Canticle* the "Bride sees herself set, and in the security...of the nuptial chamber of union with her Spouse...she sees herself set and in security."[3] "The soul is so strong and so victorious with the virtues that she has there...that the devil not only dares not approach her but flees very far from her in great terror, and dares not even appear... the soul has completely put him to flight and conquered him so that he appears no longer before her."[4]

So from the earlier quotations it seems that in the attenuated or intermittent state of union the devil has considerable nuisance-value (as will be seen in the chapter following), but in the plenary unitive life the devil has no longer to be taken into account. The soul, in this theory, is, at each stage of union, impervious to seduction. Against this view it might be advanced that free will, one of God's greatest gifts to man, ceases at some point to be operative. Can it be that just when God's gifts are reaching their fullest peak in the mystical life, this one gift which has brought the soul so far along the way of surrendering to grace need function no longer? Would God value a soul which from now on could only be a winner more than he would value a soul which could still turn out to be a loser? On the principle of no-testing, no-prize, it could surely be assumed that right up to the end there is a slight chance—the slightest possible chance in view of all the graces the soul is now enjoying in its unitive state—that fallen nature might yet make one final bid for independence.

If Lucifer was as united to God as an archangel can be and failed in his allegiance it must have meant that it was a case of free will being turned in the wrong direction. We do not know as much about angelic free will as we do about human free will, but if we know anything at all about free will we must agree with the psalmist's *anima mea in manibus meis semper*, my soul is in my hands at all times (Ps. 118:109). Adam had to be tested in the use of his free will and he failed,

---

[2] *Dark Night*, Bk. 2, ch. 20:5.
[3] *Canticle*, stan. 14, repeated in stan. 24.
[4] *Canticle*, stan 49:3.

losing his unique union with God along with his innocence and integrity. Certainly it would keep us more on the alert if we could be warned authoritatively that we are never, even in the mystical way, entirely safe. When we pray in the Mass that God may "keep us from sin" would it not be presumptuous to believe that there might come a time in our spiritual lives when this prayer need no longer apply?

But the opinion put forward here is only a private one, and if censorship opposes it, with or without a better logic, it is willingly withdrawn.

CHAPTER 14
Final Apprenticeship

BY CAUSING THE SOUL TO PASS through the final night of the spirit God draws it from the state of the proficient to the state of the perfect. These may be only badges to be noted by the director but they have their value. St. Teresa did not despise such labels and was not above tracing the soul's progress from one mansion to another. It was in her seventh mansion, it may be remembered, that she was granted the vision of the Blessed Trinity. Even in this exalted unitive life, whether graced by mystical phenomena or not, there are differing degrees, ranging it would seem from those experienced by souls whose lives are cast among people to those whose lives could be classified as contemplative. In the first group you would find St. Thomas, St. Dominic, St. Francis, St. Bonaventure, St. Ignatius, St. Francis of Sales. In the second, St. Benedict, St. Bruno, St. John of the Cross, St. Peter of Alcantara. Not that there is any competition here, or that it matters one bit to which group the particular soul belongs; the whole issue turns on the question of vocation. If St. Joan of Arc had tried to be a St. Gertrude she would probably have ended up a neurotic. If St. Thérèse of Lisieux had worked in a leper colony she might have helped a lot of lepers but her doctrine of the "little way" would not have had the influence which has turned out to be perhaps greater than any other spiritual book of the century.

It is reassuring to find in St. Thomas that the life of union which is the state of the "perfect" consists in nothing more than the "desire above all things to cleave to God and to enjoy him, and yearn ardently for eternal life and to be everlastingly with Christ."[1] St. Thomas, following Dionysius, gives what he calls the three "movements" of contemplation which correspond to the three stages described under the headings Purgative, Illuminative, Unitive. Where the beginner contemplates the goodness of God reflected in creation, where the proficient contemplates the goodness of God reflected in intelligible truth, the perfect contemplates God's goodness *in itself*. This gives us a new aspect of the conclusions arrived at and taught by St. John of the Cross. For St. Thomas the state of union is marked by the soul's prayer going around again and again in an ever increasing knowledge of truth. Christ, Truth itself, is at once the inspiration and object of this movement. The soul understands it better and comes to live by it more completely. With the deeper knowledge of divine truth comes inevitably a clearer appreciation of divine beauty.

In case this question has never been raised before, what of the good sincere people who have never come across St. Thomas, St. John of the Cross, Dionysius, the *Cloud* and the rest of the great mystical writers? (They probably know about St. Teresa of Avila as having reputedly said that we pray better when sitting down and in a comfortable position. St. Thérèse of Lisieux they know from statues and pictures.) They know nothing of the classical divisions and subdivisions. They feel that the whole subject of contemplation with its dark nights is beyond them. They have never put much store in spiritual direction, and they have confined their serious reading to lives of the saints and meditations on the Gospels. Do such souls ever arrive at the kind of profound interior prayer we have been considering, and if so, how? If not, can spirituality stand up against the charge of being selective, esoteric? A parallel could be seen in the case of people visiting a foreign country while not knowing the language. They enjoy all that others who do know the language enjoy, but if they were able to make their needs known by speaking to the natives they would be able to travel farther, faster, and get more out of their meetings with the people of the country.

[1]II-II, q. 24, a. 9.

Take the majority of good practicing Christians. They pray, are obedient to the Church, deny themselves, refer their decisions to the guidance of the Holy Spirit, try to be kind to others for the love of God. They are unpretentious, judging themselves to be inferior to their more spiritual friends. They commit the ordinary sins which they would like to correct but somehow never manage it. They are not quite sinners and not, by a long way, saints. But they are attracted to sanctity, as they are attracted to prayer. It is just that the ways of the spirit have never been explained to them. What they do not suspect for a moment is that God may be working as powerfully to bring them to union as he is in those who have the book at their fingertips and are checking themselves against the charts. Since this kind of well-intentioned but rather vague kind of person is not taken into account by mystical writers it may be helpful to see how they are placed in God's plan, and to speculate upon how they may reach the higher levels of the spirit—sometimes even without their knowing it.

The secret of it is a mixture of humility, unselfconscious fidelity, a longing to practice a better charity, and the habit of taking God at his word. This is not such an exceptional program after all, calling for perseverance rather than intelligence, rather than what we mean by devotion. On the foundation of humility the virtue of trust is built up. Given trust, there is surrender to the unrestricted way of grace. Without noticing the difference, the soul is open to the first graces of prayer and then to those that are infused. What the soul notices is that prayer becomes simpler, less methodical, less strained, more of a habit and less of a duty—no introspection, complete dependence on grace.

Accompanying this interior activity there may not be much planned mortification, but God sees to it that acceptance of the sufferings of life is becoming more instinctive and wider in application. Since the initial surrender is not withdrawn, the acceptance extends to even minor annoyances and disappointments. The full implication of the cross may not yet be grasped, and only a notional assent may be given to the value of asceticism, but the point of penance and the need for it will come with the granting of further light.

We are not describing here a "natural," a soul with the mind of a child, but a person who has chosen to be for God and who is acting according to his lights. He is in fact getting more lights than he knows about. If the process is not quite ordinary it means in effect that God is supplying for the spiritual knowledge that the person would acquire from other sources and is doing the direction himself. *Dominus solus dux ejus fuit* (Dt. 32:12), the Lord alone is his guide. The kind of person envisaged here is not an altogether unlikely one. A number of future saints must have started out like that. St. Margaret Mary and St. Bernadette certainly did. Probably St. Zita, St. Germaine ("whose only book was her rosary"), and St. Lydwine as well.

But we are not thinking here of saints so much as of souls who would get further and faster in the ways of the spirit if these ways were put to them. St. Teresa says that for a soul who is lacking a director when direction is really necessary there is no need to worry: either the light will be provided directly by God or a suitable director will come along. Again it is a question of faith. The will to do God's will, in whatever way it shows itself, is the surest indication that the light will come. Where God withholds his light it is almost always because the soul is not detached enough to act on what it shows. If the soul only knew, it is in its own interest to be kept in the dark. If the light were to come and the soul were to turn away from it then the darkness would be better than the light. God is patient. He can afford to wait until the soul is free of its own will before he makes clear what is his own. The stranger in the foreign land has to pick up the language as best he can, but though his travels will not be wasted if he does not say a word, the best way of keeping to the right roads is at least to pay the country the compliment of buying a map and a phrase book. While God does not feel bound to go by St. John of the Cross and the others, he usually puts the writers that are best for us in our way. And if he does not he gives us the feel of what should be done next. It may not always lead as far as the state of union but there is no reason why it should not.

There was once an old and rather difficult nun called Sister Agatha. (This is not a true story but it well might be.) As a young religious she was smiling, obliging, popular with the sisters, full of fun. She was also very devout, spending much of her free time in the chapel with books of devotion, litanies, and novena prayers. After profession she became less vivacious, apt to snap at people. The sisters said, "How Sister

Agatha has changed." Her superior put her to teaching in the school but this did not work for long because either she fooled about with the children as if she were their own age or else she got angry with them for no reason. She hated herself for her faults which she saw only too clearly and did penance for them to an exaggerated degree.

By now she was bored with her manuals of devotion, her litanies, her novenas, but had nothing to put in their place. So she sat about in the chapel feeling it to be the most complete waste of time. Withdrawing more and more into herself, and relieved now of school work, she was given the job of making and mending habits. This she did not like very much but it gave her a workroom to herself, and for many years she seemed to be more content—not as jolly as before but placidly content. Her great penance was community recreation at which she either expressed her opinions too forcibly, and this caused her the deepest distress afterwards, or else she sulked and said nothing, which gave her even greater cause for self-disgust. She could see her contemporaries becoming holier, better religious and more likeable as people, while she saw herself as getting worse.

In chapel she still could not pray—the convent chaplain had been no help here and she did not like to ask her superior about something which presumably she should have mastered years ago—so she fell back on the well, do-your-best formula. She had no idea what her best ought to be, or how to go about doing it. It was noticed by the others in the chapel, who were occupied by their examens and spiritual exercises, that Sister Agatha did a lot of crying.

As the years wore on Sister Agatha became arthritic in both hands, and the work of sewing grew to be too much for her. She was put on to sending out appeals for the missions, but what with her arthritic fingers and now failing sight the envelopes she addressed often failed to reach their destination. What humiliated her even more was an increasing deafness. Her hearing aid became more of an enemy than a friend.

The next stage was the wheelchair, and though she could propel herself about inside the convent she needed another sister to steer her and see that she did not roll off the paths when out of doors. The younger sisters took it in turn to perform this service, and it must be admitted that they cared for it not at all. "Sister Agatha was in a bad mood today," a junior would be heard to remark. "Sister Agatha insisted on coming back the long way, and it meant a rush to be in time for Vespers." "It's not very amusing when Sister Agatha doesn't say a word from start to finish." Sister Agatha was no fool; she knew she was being a trial to the young ones and in confession she reproached herself bitterly for it.

One day when it was a certain Sister Ruth's turn to do the pushing, Sister Agatha resolved beforehand not to be demanding or scolding but to be sweetly grateful throughout the twenty minute run. But half way through she heard herself say: "Take me over the little bridge, Sister, I want to see how the water lilies are doing this year." "It is going to rain in a minute," Sister Ruth said gently, and she was not making it up about the rain because the clouds were blackening, "don't you think we should go back the short way?" "No," said Sister Agatha, "I don't." Obediently Sister Ruth wheeled the chair towards the little bridge in the middle of which she was commanded to halt. Just as they were close to the parapet the sun burst between the clouds and they were able to see their reflections in the water below. "Am I really so old and irritable-looking?" sighed Sister Agatha. "Let's get back as quickly as we can." Sister Ruth who had been looking only at her own reflection—the way one instinctively does—decided to take a quick look at Sister Agatha's. What she saw looking up at her from the surface of the water was the most beautiful face she had ever seen in her life.

While there are several points relating to the actual exercise of prayer on which mystical writers are found to differ—for example whether the work of the intellect or the will plays the more important part while praying; what would be the signs of changing from a lower to a higher form of prayer; does faith while in the dark night allow a return to a lower form of prayer or does it demand that one hang on and wait for a clearer indication as to how to proceed; must one suppress the impulse to invoke Mary and the saints while contemplating or may one give in to it without scruple; if not bound by vow to the recitation of the Divine Office may one suspend its habitual use for a time and spend the equivalent hours in meditative reading—and differ a lot of them do, there is one thing they are all agreed upon and that is that the prayer of full union cannot be arrived at except by way of the last of the nights, the nature of which is more crushing than any of the earlier ones.

We are talking now of the final, most productive, most sacrificial, most rewarding apprenticeship. The time it takes may be long or short depending on how successfully it is endured. What Garrigou-Lagrange calls "the third conversion" and St. John of the Cross calls "the painful crisis of the passive purgation of the spirit" is necessary before the soul can come totally to the life of union. For once St. John of the Cross is misleading in his use of the word "beginners" which we naturally associate with the Purgative Way. He mentions beginners again when describing the dark night of the spirit. Since this cannot mean that the neophyte plunges straight from his first experience of the spiritual life into the mystical state which is passively preparing for union, it must mean that St. John is referring to those who are beginning on the last lap.

However painful we feel the time of preparation we have to believe that the Resurrection would not have taken place without Good Friday. Purgatory (for most of us anyway) is a necessary prelude to heaven. Even worldly people know that the good things of life do not come to us on oiled runners but have to be paid for. It is one of the laws of legend as well as one of the laws of life. Sleeping Beauty is surrounded by thorns, not by lilies and birds of many colors. The eternal flame is kept alight not by virgins with tambourines but by witches muttering curses. The alarms surrounding Fort Knox electrocute even bees and mosquitoes. The tabernacle of the Blessed Sacrament is safeguarded by the threat of sacrilege and excommunication. The higher the good the higher the price. Descriptions of the night which give place to the light of union may be boring, but unless their significance is grasped it is no good hoping that an academic interest in the mystical life will bring one to the experience of ultimate union. St. John of the Cross, St. Teresa, Dionysius, the *Cloud*, St. Thomas, Hugh of St. Victor are not just experts in their field, literary trailblazers, they are authorities of flesh and blood and soul who could explain their experience in the way they did so that we in our fumbling search might find echoes of help. Think of their dark nights not so much as warnings scaring you off but as circumstances to be ready for. If suffering is not a punishment it is an opportunity. (The word "challenge" has been overworked but that is what suffering is meant to be.)

From the *Imitation* to the latest book about the ascetical life there is the exhortation to rejoice in tribulation. Nothing wrong with this—we should joyfully make the most of the horrors that beset our lives—but we cannot do this simply by making up our minds. Nothing but faithful correspondence with the grace of the Holy Spirit in the life of prayer can, as St. Teresa repeatedly claims, bring about this disposition. Consequently it is only the willingness to go all the way in love and trust that can call down upon the soul the supreme grace of mystical union with God.

Theology tells us that the pain of hell, and to a lesser degree, that of purgatory, is essentially that of loss—loss of God together with the knowledge that one has lost him through one's own fault. This particular kind of agony is reflected in the dark night of the spirit. The soul in hell really has lost God, and forever, while of course the soul in the dark night has not only not lost God but is in the process of finding him. Compared with the soul in purgatory the soul in the dark night suffers the added agony of feeling that the loss *is* forever; the soul in purgatory has at least the knowledge that there will be an end of its misery and that God will reveal himself when the time of purgation has done its work. Describing the dark night Thomas Merton used the word "anguish" which would seem to go further than "agony"—we think of agony as something more connected with the body, and as something which can be expected eventually to pass. Anguish is something essentially in the mind, mixed up with dread and anxiety—something very near to despair. This is exactly what the dark night of the soul is.

The homesick child cannot imagine a future when there will not be homesickness. Prometheus, chained to his rock, believes he will be there forever. The bedridden invalid does not expect to live any other kind of life. The darkest of dark nights has all this and more—more because the soul is convinced that it has deserved the punishment it is getting. If regret is one of the main elements in the soul's condition in hell and purgatory, it is equally a large part of the soul's suffering in the dark night. Indeed it can become *too* much a part of the soul's suffering at this stage. Remorse can, carried beyond a certain point, leave too little room for trust. It is to the act of total trust that the challenge of the dark night is directed. Compunction, inspired as it is by love, has a cleansing effect; remorse, which is self-regarding, is to some degree an act of atonement but if it is to have any supernatural value must be filial rather than servile. It must be raised, through sorrow for sin, to an act of love for the one sinned against. Souls have been known to spend longer in the dark night than they need have done because they have handled negatively qualities of mind and heart which they could have handled positively by directing them towards the love of God.

St. John of the Cross enumerates imperfections of which the soul may be guilty even at this late stage, and which have to be got rid of before finally being admitted to union. What he calls "natural rough-ness" is one of them, and it can be seen how, while enduring so many tensions, a person may well be less agreeable than he might be. What is going on in his soul is also going on in his nerves, and perhaps not until he reaches the peace and joy of union will his nervous system be able to simmer down. The genuine fully fledged mystic will show no "natural roughness" but, on the contrary, be as amiable as can be.

Presumption is another of the obstacles to the final dawn. In view of all the self-loathing and self-recrimination which have made the darkness so much worse it is difficult to see how this particular evil can assert itself, but St. John says that in certain natures it does, so we must bow to his judgment.

The attempt to hang onto earlier forms of prayer, earlier experien-ces of God's favor, is more understandable. In desperation, even in natural emergencies, we instinctively try to remember how we man-aged to get out of our troubles before. Now, in the emergency of near-despair, the soul casts about for the securities of an earlier time. To cling to a memory is pardonable enough but a habit to be guarded against. God granted a particular kind of security at one stage in the soul's education and is giving another more secret kind now. Souls should not confuse their securities one with another—that grace for then, this grace for now. New wine should not be poured into old wineskins, or old into new. The fact that the present grace cannot be felt, whereas the older one was, makes the present grace all the more profitable. *Memor fui dierum antiquorum,* "I recall the days of old, I reflect on all that you did, I ponder your deeds; I stretch out my hands, like thirsty ground I yearn for you. Quick, Lord, answer me before my spirit fails; if you hide your face much longer, I shall go down to the pit like the rest. Let dawn bring proof of your love" (Ps. 143:5-8). Certainly the psalmist knew this aspect of the night, and if further evidence of this is needed, the whole of Psalm 88 (87) should be read. It is the only psalm in the entire psalter which contains not a gleam of joy.

As a tailpiece to the list of harmful tendencies as given by St. John of the Cross, the "purging virtues" mentioned by St. Thomas[2] may be mentioned here. "Prudence despises the things of the world in favor of the contemplation of divine things." This relates to the Purgative Way. "Prudence moreover directs all thoughts to God." This would be a characteristic of the Illuminative Way. "Temperance gives up all that the body demands so far as nature can allow." So this virtue would seem to be needed at every stage of the journey, even after union has been reached. "Fortitude prevents us from fearing either death or the unknown element belonging to higher states." Again this is a virtue applicable to each stage but particularly to the later dark nights. "Justice finally makes us enter fully into the way of God." Evidently St. Thomas is thinking of a special kind of justice, not the judicial kind, which reveals to the mind the reasonableness of taking on the spiritual life and all that it may entail. When he talks about the state of union he drops all mention of his four classical categories, and speaks only of charity.

A mistaken approach, not mentioned by St. John of the Cross but one which must even more get in the way of final union, is one which might clumsily be called the non-anthropomorphic. As many books as ever are being written about our Lord, and this is of course good so

---

[2] I-II, q. 51, a. 5.

long as they are in accordance with traditional Catholic teaching, but where it comes to the spiritual life, especially in its higher reaches of mysticism, there is something felt to be significantly lacking. There are books which say a lot about God and love and the need for acceptance, but they seem to leave out Christ. Partly this could be accounted for by the modern tendency to canonize Eastern philosophy and religion and partly because people are more interested, with the spread of psychiatry, in finding themselves than in finding Christ. If our Christian mysticism is to be authentic, indeed if our prayer life from the very beginning is to be safe, it must be incarnational.

So let this section be introduced by a quotation from St. Irenaeus where he says, "Wherefore the Word passed through every stage of life, restoring all to communion with God."[3] A case could be made out, indeed has been made out, by popular non-Catholic theologians, that prayer which has Christ as its focus is a misunderstanding not only of true mysticism but of the Incarnation itself. In such a view a Christ-orientated spirituality humanizes the transcendent mystery of God. In such a view it does not bring humanity into union with God but brings divinity down to the level of man. Leaving definitions to the experts, we would do well to remember that St. Athanasius, Doctor of the Church, has said, "God became man that man might become God."[4] It has further been suggested by historians belonging to the same school that medieval mystics such as Eckhart, Tauler, Hugh of St. Victor, Ruysbroeck, and Denis the Carthusian made little of the place of the sacred humanity in contemporary mysticism. Lists of names can never be very convincing but at least the argument can be countered with those of St. Teresa, St. Bernard, St. Bonaventure ("the crucifix is my authority"), St. Gertrude, St. Angela of Foligno. Then there is the evidence of the stigmata, proving, if anything does, the validity of Christo-centric spirituality. More than three hundred cases of the stigmata cannot be dismissed.

All this has been dragged in, not as a piece of theological controversy, but simply to warn souls against the advice to keep their prayer

[3] *Contra haer.*, 3. 18. 7.
[4] *De Incarn. Verbi*, 54;3.

as abstract as possible and to banish from it the thought of Christ. This idea of the Quietists has been condemned by the Church.

For souls who are enduring the dark nights Christ's words about his own dark night may be for them the only comfort. "It was for this that I came unto this hour" (Jn. 12:27). "Father, save me from this hour" (Jn. 12:27). The chapters in St. John's Gospel which tell of our Lord's discourse to his disciples are full of the contrast between darkness and light, sorrow and joy, and always the need for trust. "Whosoever believes in me need not stay in the dark forever" (Jn. 12:46).

He gives us everything to look forward to, but while in our present state we cannot appreciate what he is holding out to us. "I am going now to prepare a place for you; after I have gone I shall return" (Jn. 14:2-3). "Make your home in me as I have made my home in you" (Jn. 15:4). "Unless I go, the Advocate will not come to you" (Jn. 16:7). "In a short while you will not see me, and in a short while you will see me again" (Jn. 16:16).

How is it that the soul longs for God as never before and yet cannot take in what he says? "You will be sorrowful but your sorrow will be turned into joy... I shall see you again and your hearts shall be full of joy, and that joy none shall take from you" (Jn. 16:22).

Yet knowing all this he could say hardly an hour later, "Save me from this hour... Lord, if it be possible let this chalice pass from me, yet not my will be done... my God, my God, why have you forsaken me?" (Jn. 12:27; Mt. 27:45). The vindication of the mystery came at the last moment: "Into your hands I commend my spirit" (Mt. 27:50). The dark night had done its work. Now came the recognition of the union which had in fact never been interrupted. For our part it is in the trust born of Christ's experience that our time of waiting must lie.

Whatever mysticism is for the Hindu, the Buddhist, the Confucinist, for us it is simply Christ—the ever deeper indwelling of him in us and we in him. St. Paul knew this better than anyone: for him to live was Christ and he had no life outside of Christ. In Christ who strengthened him, St. Paul knew he could do all things, the implication being that without Christ's strength he could do nothing. Without his grace, St. Paul says, we cannot even call upon his name. For him, as for mankind at large, salvation rests upon Jesus Christ yesterday, today, and the same forever.

If Christian mysticism is Christ, is as we have seen "incarnational," it is also sacramental. Souls who imagine that their lofty mystical state entitles them to dispense with the Eucharist are no Christian mystics; they are deluded by the devil who is today more than ever trying to downplay the sacraments. Whether in the dark night or enjoying the interludes in between, souls need Holy Communion and the sacrament of penance. More than ever in the advanced stages of contemplation the soul has to rely upon the Church's sacramental life. How far contemplatives, when in the dark night, *feel* the good of the sacraments is another matter; the point is they recognize their necessity.

It is the work of grace that those who suffer the worst of all afflictions—the belief that they have deserted God and that God has deserted them—are nevertheless faithful to the full observance of religion. They may tell you it is only because they "have been brought up that way" or that merely "going through the motions" cannot be doing either themselves or God any good. But they cling all the same with a tenacity which they would not dream of showing where interests apart from religion were concerned. A man who loses all interest in music does not go to concerts, a painter who turns to mechanics will come to look upon an exhibition of pictures as a waste of time. In the spiritual life, however darkened and made miserable by the sense of guilt, it is grace that is the pull.

Perseverance in obeying the demands of the Church does not of itself produce love. We are always being warned against a lifeless routine. But perseverance for the sake of a love of which the soul is not sensibly aware does produce love, *is* in fact love. It is this love which is being tested in the dark night. God is love, and it is his love working in us that produces our love for him.

One of the surprising facts about the experience of the dark night (though it is not so surprising when you see the reason for it) is that when souls look for relief and comfort in the direction where they might legitimately expect the answers they are looking for, namely in such texts as have been quoted above and in the works of writers such as St. John of the Cross, the relief they get is only momentary or not at all. They read the words, they know the words must be true, but they remain largely deaf to their application. The explanation is that without a light of some sort you cannot read a book in the dark. If the night of the spirit is to do its work of purification and preparation it must be completely dark. Once again a man may give as a reason for his noncomprehension his spiritual insensitiveness, his worthlessness. "God means these things for other people, not for me." God means them for him all right, and the time will come when the man's eyes will be opened and he will know that they applied so closely to his case that they might have been spoken individually to him as though there had been nobody else in the world. But this is to anticipate the subject of the next and final chapter.

Meanwhile what is the course to adopt? Trust, of course, as we have insisted all along. So a better question to ask would be what course not to adopt. Suppose you have a dog which is dying of cancer. The dog knows it is suffering but attributes the cause to a splinter which has got into one of its paws. He worries about his splinter and tries by every means to get it out. His limping, his melancholy expression and obvious discomfort arouses someone's sympathy, and on examination the splinter is removed. The dog thinks that this means the end of his misery and goes off wagging its tail. But the cancer remains. The moral of the story is that we tend to confuse the causes of our misery. We think that a change of job would put us right, that to go away for a year would make all the difference, that the climate is against us, that we must have some allergy which we do not know about but which is making life unbearable, that we were born neurotics and that the signs of it are only showing themsevles now. We are thinking of splinters in paws. It is to the affliction which God is sending us, which he is allowing as a privilege, that we must adapt ourselves.

"Keep your attention closely on it," says St. Peter in his second Epistle, "as you would on a lamp shining in a dark place, until the first streaks of dawn appear and the morning star rises in your hearts" (2 Pt. 1:19).

CHAPTER 15
Consummation

MOST SPIRITUAL WRITERS WOULD AGREE that the soul's first experience of the Unitive Way, the dark night of the spirit now behind it, is the sense of profound humility. One prefers here to write if possible of the apostles and their reactions rather than of the free lance authors, however accredited, and of their reported accounts. Take St. Paul who proclaimed at once that it was by the grace of God that he was what he was and not by any merit of his own. The grace in him had not been void. He had not forced it, he had given in to it. His union with God had made him realize that he was nothing and that God was all, that his greatest strength lay in his infirmity. Once he could honestly acknowledge his weakness then God would come in to make him strong. "The weak things has God chosen to confound the strong; the foolish of this world to confound the wise" (1 Cor. 1:20). For the rest of the apostles it was the same—they were nothing of themselves. They needed Pentecost to be strong enough to do the job. Hitherto they had, in their various degrees, aspired to this or that form of service. Now, with union, they found themselves knowing what to do and strong enough to do it.

It was the same with Mary Magdalen. Conscious of her sinful past, she prided herself on nothing. Love obliterated all that, and it was Christ's love working itself out in her that put her at the foot of the cross, at the empty tomb, in the garden.

In line with the apostles and Mary Magdalen, the Christian mystic admits that, in spite of himself, of his unworthiness, of his sinful past, he has been picked up through no merit of his own by grace and called to union. False mystics are of a quite different mind. They glory not in their infirmities but in their strength, in their determination to win through to the topmost positions in the spiritual hierarchy. They believe that sanctity is something they can force, that prayer is not so much infused as induced. Lacking the infused prayer of the Illuminative Way they experiment with artificial means in bringing about what they hope will be the same result. If true union is to be denied them, they would be willing to settle for second best whatever the ways of getting there. The devil is only too willing to oblige.

Whether classified as the active or passive state of union, the condition is essentially within. It is helped by, and verified by, the outward means chosen to come by the state of union, but the outward is only the reflection of the inward. Natural will power, aided by grace, makes a good start, but in the last analysis the story is not told by the natural will but by the natural will informed by the supernatural action of grace. When this is acknowledged by the soul, and is not merely a proposition to which a notional consent is given, humility is the result. This is why the first sign of union is the awareness of nothingness, and the awareness of the all.

Take the case of a nature lover, but one with sharp preferences and prejudices. (Not that it is of any consequence but this time it is a true story.) He delights in the sea, provided it is not noisy with waves, and with gently flowing streams. He likes nothing better than mountains, provided he does not have to climb them, because they soothe his spirit by their immobility, they iron out the knotted surface of his ever agitated nature. Mountain towns come and go, the sun scorches them, frosts crack their boulders, fires and gales destroy their trees, but the shapes remain for centuries and he likes that. Plants, shrubs, flowers and giant trees he loves, except when they are arranged as part of a planned landscape. He gets on with most animals. Birds he cannot abide. Stars and the skies bore him since as a young man he had studied astronomy. Then one night he was praying and he happened to look up at the heavens. It was not his custom to pray out of doors, especially at night, but on this occasion, washed by recent rains, he saw Andromeda, Orion, Cassiopeia as if for the first time. He was conscious of looking six billion years into the past. He did not have to remember about the relative positions of the various galaxies. He did not have to calculate when, according to the speed of light, what he was seeing had left its particular star or planet. He forgot everything about the science of astronomy but was conscious of two great lights in his soul which were brighter than any star. The first showed him that in the context of so much time he was smaller than a grain of sand, the second was that he was more loved by God than anything skies could show him, and closer to God because God was inside him and because he was inside God. God was in all his creation (not in a pantheistic sense) as a sculptor is in his works, but not in the way that he was in him. To have a taste for nature is the same as having a taste for anything else—for classical music, caviar, the Impressionists, the ballet—but to learn a spiritual truth from a natural taste is a grace.

Both nature and grace are God's gifts to man, but just as we have not merited the beauties of nature, we have not merited grace however hard we have worked for it. Nature is an outside gift, grace an inside one. The popular idea that the saints have risen to sanctity by their own effort can be corrected by the strictly theological truth that we cannot start off on the way to sanctity unless God is already inside us inspiring us to make the effort. The indwelling of God in the soul is something actual which we come gradually to realize, not something which we arrive at by obeying the rules.

Meister Eckhart, for all his sometimes extravagant opinions which got him into trouble, was perfectly orthodox in his understanding of this truth. "I do not find God outside myself nor conceive him excepting as my own and in me," he wrote. "A man ought to work only for that which is his being, his very life within him."[1] And again: "The eye with which I see God is the same eye with which God sees me. My eye and God's eye is one eye, is one sight, is one knowledge, is one love." Wrongly understood, the Eckhart doctrine could be interpreted as meaning that we need not look for God in people, in suffering, in the Church. In fact, though he was fully vindicated in the end and his orthodoxy established, the Eckhart doctrine was so interpreted. What he meant was, and this is where it affects our present consideration of

---

[1] *Meister Eckhart* by Pfeiffer, vol. 1, p. 163.

the prayer of union, that it is only in virtue of our union with God, begun in baptism, that the Unitive Way can be understood at all, much less experienced.

Reading the mystics is not like reading the psychologists, or even the philosophers. It is as if you had to keep three eyes open at once: with your theological eye you have to judge the truth of what your psychological and philosophical eyes show you. Only so can your mystical eye, now the fourth on the list, look ahead without the distraction of argument.

If humility can be instanced as the first resulting effect of the grace of transforming union, the sense of spiritual freedom might be given as the second.[2] Not freedom from the rules of the Church, from tradition, from cramping methods of prayer, but freedom at last from *self*. Though St. Paul may not be referring specifically to the unitive state in its mystical context, the closing verse of the eighth chapter of his Letter to the Romans describes exactly the sense of liberation, of a new-found intimacy with Christ, of complete trust in the providence of God with regard to whatever lies in store. "I am certain of this," he says, "neither death nor life, no angel, no prince, nothing that exists, nothing still to come, not any power, nor height nor depth, nor any created thing, can ever come between us and the love of God made visible in Christ Jesus our Lord" (Rom. 8:38-39). Self-interest has fallen away, dropped like a stone into the dirty pool of the past. To change the metaphor it is as if a bird which has been pinioned since it left the nest suddenly discovers the joy of unweighted flight. The hook has been taken from the salmon's mouth and it can leap upstream, downstream, or any way it chooses.

A new meaning is given to de Caussade's "sacrament of the present moment." The past is over and done with; what matters is the *now* which has the quality of a revelation. The future is there but is not dreaded anymore, it is simply not envisaged. A person in good health does not wonder as he is going to bed whether he will be able to sleep

---

[2]Alan Watts, in the thought-provoking book, *Behold the Spirit*, gives a different priority. His book is significant from many points of view, his reading wide and eclectic.

well or not—he takes the night for granted as he has taken the day for granted. The sacrament of the present moment is the meeting of God's moment, which is eternal, with the soul's moment, which is not recorded on any clock so is eternal also in union with the eternity of God.

If time does not matter anymore, neither does space. There is still the necessary *here* and *there*, but the environment in which places exist is the environment of God's ubiquitous presence. He is in all, with all, through all. There is nowhere where he is not, and just as he is living at all times within the united soul so he is living at all times in the universe which has not so much come *out* of the divine mind as has never left it.

Before the state of union was reached the soul knew periods of peace and joy. The emotions were real enough as far as they went, and they were recognized as coming from God and were received with thanksgiving. But now they are possessed at a different level. Hitherto there usually had to be a reason for joy—a meeting with someone loved, a sense of well-being as the result of having carried off a work successfully, a piece of good news, the unexpected reversal of a disappointment—but now there does not have to be any particular reason because the cause of the joy is the joy of God which the soul is being granted to share.

Now this is no speculation of the mystics. This is Christ's promise and guarantee. "I have told you this," Christ says, "so that my own joy may be in you and your joy may be complete" (Jn. 15:11). "That your sorrow [the dark night] may be turned into joy" (Jn. 16:20). "I shall be with you again and your hearts will be full of joy and that joy *no one shall take from you*" (Jn. 16:22). In union the soul's joy will be analogous to, but in its nature exceeding, anything it has ever experienced before. This is not surprising when we consider that it is not the soul's personally experienced joy but Christ's—not one's own but his shared.

Peace in the same way. "*My* peace I give unto you"—not any old kind of peace which by adroit maneuvering you can bring about. It has to be Christ's peace or it is no more than placidity and calm. In the Unitive Way it simply comes: it is not fought for, not adroitly planned, not hedged against possible interference. It comes as a consequence of union with the peace of Christ. In fact it is his, not ours. "*My* peace I give you," not the world's, not the absence of strife, not the tranquility which is threatened by unexpected disaster, not the contrived peace of the Greeks or the imposed peace of the Romans, not the political and artificial peace hoped for by the United Nations, but the peace of Christ. In spite of the cloud of the Passion under which Christ lived, in spite of the opposition he received from his own, in spite of the turbulence of the first Holy Week, even in spite of his sense of desolation and desertion by the Father on Calvary, somehow or other —somewhere in the pinnacle of his spirit which is a mystery which we cannot understand—Christ knew peace. If he did not, then his union with the Father, affirmed by the doctrine of the Blessed Trinity, is without meaning.

In the Unitive state, the virtue of love, which cannot be different in character from what it has always been taught to be, assumes new depths, dimension, and application. It is, of course, a commandment because our Lord said it was, and indeed is the greatest of the commandments. But now, in the Unitive Way, it is less of a duty superimposed and more of an expression spontaneously expressed. The soul now realizes that the first commandment could not be anything else. It is the greatest commandment because God is the greatest exponent of love. He *is* love. To live in God is to live in love, to live in love is to live in God. It seems so logical, so simple. Yet for all of us it is the virtue we practice least. Even in the Unitive Way, when you would expect the soul to be so identified with him who is love itself that it would be above uncharitableness, there still remains what theologians call the *fomes peccati*, and among these are occasional wayward expressions of self-sufficiency, rash judgment, comparison with those less fortunate or even with such a natural failing as irritation with those who impose on one. We are never quite free of original sin and its consequences.

Obedience and forgiveness in the Unitive Way are absolutes, as indeed they should be in every way, and so need no elaboration here. But impatience, laziness, self-indulgence, and desire for reciprocated affection admit of degrees and are with us until the end of our days.

Unitive prayer is not magic, nor is it the kind of mental operation which extracts once and for all the nasty tendencies we are born with. Some people are congenitally impatient, and the only difference which their transforming union makes is to give them greater graces of self-control. As regards laziness, lack of mortification, romantic attachment with useless daydreams, the light which comes with union warns souls of their danger, opens their eyes to their occasions, and turns their energies into more positive and spiritual directions. In building up and perfecting the spiritual life, grace never eliminates nature but redirects it. Something of the fallen ego, not much of it if the soul has truly yielded to the grace of transformation, remains. In a way perhaps it is well that this is so: it confirms the soul's newly discovered humility and at the same time disguises from others the more than ordinary working of grace.

So much for the influence of union on conduct and the quality of the soul's virtue. Now for the more important influence on the soul's spiritual perceptions. Commenting on John 14:23, the authority whom we have been mostly considering, namely St. John of the Cross, has this to say: "This, namely 'On that day you will understand that I am in my Father, and you in me and I in you,' means that the soul's understanding will be divinely enlightened by the wisdom of the Son, that his will will be filled with delight by the Holy Spirit, and that the Father with power and strength will draw him into the unfathomable mystery of his tender love." This can only refer to mystical union. The same subject of the union of the soul with God is alluded to where he says: "We shall observe that the principal characteristic, on account of which it is here called a ladder, is that it is the science of love. This is an infused and loving knowledge of God which enlightens the soul and at the same time enkindles it with love, until it is raised up, step by step, even to God its Creator."[3]

Though he does not mention mystical union in as many words, the author of the *Cloud*, in a short treatise which editors have called *In the Image and Likeness of God*, clearly has this culminating state in mind when he says:

[3]*Dark Night*, Bk. 2:18.

There is one common will unto all three Persons. The will is good in giving of the gifts of nature unto his image, so answering to God the Father. It is well-pleasing in the giving of the gifts of grace, so answering to God the Son. And it is perfect in giving of the full and the final ending of blessedness, answering to the Holy Ghost. And therefore to this will should every true Christian man be confirmed with all his powers...the giving of blessedness, the which is the perfectest gift, finally fulfilling with perfect charity the third power of the soul, the which is the will answering to God the Holy Ghost.[4]

While it would be tedious to quote what the many authorities have written about the soul's deepening knowledge of the Blessed Trinity dwelling within the soul, St. Catherine of Siena may speak for them all when she says towards the end of her *Dialogue*: "O Eternal Trinity, O Godhead, O divine Nature that gave to the blood of your Son so great a price. Thou, O Eternal Trinity, art a bottomless sea into which the more I plunge the more I find, and the more I find the more I seek Thee still...the soul that is sated in Thy depths desires Thee yet unceasingly for it hungers ever after Thee...Thou art the fire that ever burns and is never quenched, the fire that consumes in itself *all the self-love of souls....* This light is an ocean into which the soul plunges ever more deeply and there finds peace."[5] The words "unceasingly," "hungers ever," "never quenched" may not prove but certainly imply an almost continuous experience of the presence of the Blessed Trinity. That St. John of the Cross, St. Teresa, the author of the *Cloud*, St. Catherine, St. Thomas speak of the Blessed Trinity as the climax of mystical awareness is highly significant, particularly since after what St. Thomas calls the "divine awakening,"[6] by which he means union, the soul comes to recognize more clearly the specific attributes associated with each of the divine Persons.

It is not surprising then that the soul, in so close a relationship with the Blessed Trinity, should know true joy where before it touched only joy's surface. Phrases such as "that my joy may remain in you," "your

[4]*Image and Likeness of God,* para. 3 and 4.
[5]Ch. 167.
[6]*Living Flame,* 4:3, 4, 5.

joy may be full," "your joy no man shall take from you," all from our Lord's last discourse to the apostles, set up vibrations in the mind which ring with a particular insistence and promise.

Peace in the same way becomes, after the divine awakening, a consequence of sharing in the peace of Christ. "My peace I give you, not as the world gives" (Jn. 14:27). "In me you may have peace" (Jn. 16:33). This is not to say that life from now on is uninterrupted bliss. It is to say that deep down in the soul joy and peace have become, between them, an established habit. It is a habit which knows what to do with doubt, loneliness, fear. It is proof against resentment, envy. It accepts in all the circumstances and contingencies of the day the providential will of God. Behind everything that happens, and also behind everything the soul wants to happen but which in fact does not happen, is the love of God. Always it is St. Paul's matchless flash of autobiography: "In whatsoever state I am, I am content therewith" (Phil. 4:11), or Mary's "Be it to me according to your word" (Lk. 1:38).

Mention has been made of the sense of freedom experienced in the Unitive Way, and since misconstruction here has led to many errors, not to mention a heresy or two, it might be well to sharpen the understanding of it. Obviously it does not issue a free pass to do and say what one likes. It does not look down upon those poor conservative souls in the Purgative and Illuminative Ways who must think and act according to the handbook and itinerary. It does not canonize that "liberty of spirit" which can be made to excuse almost any departure from the accepted norm. Nor does it draw attention to its prerogatives as a chosen soul. If the sense of freedom which results from the grace of union is to be proved genuine, not one of these exaggerations may be manifest. The freedom we are thinking about is not a permission, or even in its immediate sense a privilege; it is an interior consequence of sharing the mind of Christ. Just as Christ was free from building up personal animosities, harboring antipathies, dwelling on resentments, maneuvering himself into positions which would win him praise, so does the soul feel free of such petty movements. These are a person's natural reactions, if not very agreeable ones, but the person's supernatural reactions are so strong that they count for nothing.

One of the strongest natural reactions is self-pity, so what about that after the "divine awakening"? Apart from the selfishness, the folly of it, what is there to pity self about any more? The whole scene has changed. All the soul's perspectives are different. Virtues and values are seen in their true proportions. Can you imagine Mary, counting her seven sorrows, feeling sorry for herself? She was feeling so grateful for the opportunity of suffering them that self-pity did not enter in. If one of her titles is Mother of Pity it is because, knowing sorrow, she has pity for other people, no pity for herself. It is like Dido to Aeneas: "Having known misery, I have learned how to compassionate the miserable." Her own misery was remembered only for what she could give to others. This is the liberty we are talking about.

Can you imagine St. Francis, now at the end of his life almost entirely blind, suffering in every limb, having to accept the new directions that were being given to the Order he had founded, complaining that he had been cheated of what he had set himself to do, that he felt humiliated being carried about on a litter, that his stigmata prevented his writing letters or walking barefoot? It was then that he wrote his Canticle of the Sun, and even sang it to anyone who cared to listen. This is the liberty we are talking about.

Can you imagine St. Thomas More, when he heard what his sentence was to be, saying to his daughter, Meg: "I wouldn't mind being thrown to the lions for the faith in the way that the early Christians were in Rome. That would have looked so much better in the history books. But merely to be executed for treason is not at all what I would have chosen." Instead it was "I have served my king but I serve God more." This is the liberty we are talking about.

We must not read into the happiness and peace of the Unitive Way more than it is intended to show. Always we have to bear in mind the words of our Lord, who *created* the Unitive Way: "My soul is disturbed, what shall I say?" (Jn. 12:27). Theology tells us of the divided consciousness in his divine-human mind, but the fact remains he did say these words while a part of him, the most secret part of him, was not for an instant separated from the Father. The state of union was suspended in the emotions; it was as strong as ever in the will. If it may be said with reverence, most of us have such a rosy picture of the Unitive Way that it resembles the third act of a musical. We think of our Lord welcoming the newcomer saying, "I hope you will like it here. I am in charge and will do my best to make you happy. Remember it is only the novitiate, as it were, the jumping-off state for something even better, and then what you have begun here will go on forever and ever."

For how long before her death, one wonders, was St. Thérèse of Lisieux able to *enjoy* her state of union? She was *content*, in the way that St. Paul was content as we have seen, in the state God required of her. For long before the end, however, she had to face the blackness of near-despair and the unreason of life, of meaninglessness everywhere she looked, the starkness of *le néant*. It is examples of this kind which makes one wonder about the relative amount of years, or months, spent in darkness on the one hand or in light on the other. The answer can only come from the experience of the individual, but of this we may be sure that the time factor will depend very largely on the quality of the soul concerned, on courage and generosity. Do inherited tendencies play a part, unmerited obstacles, legitimate reliefs? We do not know. All we know is that whatever the impediments, outward and physical or inward and psychological, God's grace is always there measuring out what is best for the soul and making up for the blunders.

Perhaps the best way of looking at the state of union is to look at the state of un-union or not-yet union (which after all is the state of the vast majority of those who are trying to get nearer to God in the spiritual life and failing to a greater or lesser degree), and to try to pin down the causes of failure. Each of us would have to make out his own list of the obstacles which seem to be preventing him from getting on in the spiritual life. In general it might be suggested that the areas for consideration could be reduced to lack of trust, self-absorption, instability, self-deception.

The reason that the more blatant evils of pride and uncharity have not headed the list of obstacles to spiritual progress is because it is the more subtle drawbacks that will be considered, the sins we scarcely notice, feel little compunction about, seldom mention in confession. Yet it is because we make no effort to correct them that they do the harm. Once a weakness is taken for granted, it has it all its own way. Instead of writing books about the big sins and the important virtues, someone should write a book about the small sins and the small virtues which could be magnified.

For this section it will be a help to bear in mind that four times in the Old Testament God refers to himself as a "jealous" God. The suggestion is not so much that he is jealous of the love we feel for others—though it can be that too if our love excludes the love we owe to him—but that he is jealous of whatever is apart from him in our wills. The sin he is warning us against is leaving him out, and of all the sins in the world this is the one most often committed. He is accordingly more jealous of our intentions than of our affections. We cannot help being attracted to people, and it is right that we should be, but when our affection is in deliberate competition with our service of love, and wins over, then the spiritual life, particularly the contemplative and mystical life, is held up—perhaps held up for good. Unless we are to be torn to shreds at possibly any stage in the journey towards God by the fear of being attracted by influences not immediately connected with God, we must get this point right.

God has implanted in our human nature a two-way magnetism the existence of which must be taken into account. It is as natural to feel affection as it is to feel hungry or cold. The stimuli are there, in God's created order, and we recognize this and take steps in dealing with them. However much we may wish to, for the greater love of God, we cannot spend our whole lives in flight. For one thing there is nowhere in the world to which we can fly that can guarantee our immunity. For another we are not meant to. Various sects in the course of history have tried it and it has not worked. The Christian principle is simple: we assume the existence of natural affection and raise it to the supernatural level. This is no trick; it is not just changing the labels. It is not pulling an angel out of a hat which normally contains rabbits. It is accepting a gift from God, thanking him for it, and giving it back to him who can make a better use of it than we can.

To deny the existence of affection in ourselves is to be guilty of untruth. To exploit it for physical pleasure is to offend against love in general and God's love in particular. To justify such exploitation is to offend against one's own mind, against reason, against social justice, against the order created by God.

This long preamble has been brought in to show how lack of trust, how preoccupation with self, how instability and self-deception are related in one way or another to the just jealousy of God.

First, trust. As in all virtues there are degrees of trust, but in this virtue it could be said there are two kinds of trust: trusting in God as regards circumstances and trusting in God as regards grace. Examples of the former would be to trust him in the outcome of financial difficulties, in the right choice of a job, in the use of words for a speech that has to be made, in the restoration of health. Examples of the latter would be to trust that enough grace would be given to resist temptation, to get through the dark night, to pray in the way God wants and not because one has got into a rut and has not the courage to get out of it. It is this second kind of trust which concerns us here.

The words "trust" and "hope" are often taken to mean the same thing. When we hope we are usually hoping for a particular thing, a particular solution. When we trust we are handing everything to God, and though we may be looking for a grace which will meet our need, we are confident that his wisdom is eternally at work and that we have nothing to fear. It is this kind of overall trust that interior souls know all about in theory but fail to apply to their spiritual lives in practice. It is not that they consciously bring down this spiritual trust, which is another name for faith, to a natural and psychological level. It is more that they find themselves speculating when they should be blindly sacrificing. Once we start wondering about what will happen, when it will happen, how it will happen, we are limiting the extent of our trust—we are measuring, setting boundaries. God wants our whole trust, total and not compared or weighed. In the mystical life the giving of *carte blanche* is one of the main conditions, and it is sometimes because they are shy of giving it that their prayer of union is delayed. God's "jealousy" demands that we do not ask questions about what he is doing or why. Our confidence in his wisdom means not comparing it with our own. This brings us to the next obstacle on the list.

Second, self-absorption. As will have been noticed by anyone who has got as far as this in the book, a large part of the spiritual life is spent in darkness, uncertainty, and a discouragement amounting almost to despair. "Where did I go wrong? I never used to be as awful as this. At one time I was taking one step after another, and though I didn't make as much headway as I had hoped, and as the saints in the books seemed to be making it with no more to go on than I had, I didn't worry. With unpromising material I was doing my best. But now everything has gone sour on me, and I am pretty sure I am not doing my best. What was the first mistake? All right, it was following other interests, looking for recognition and admiration. But little of that came my way so I was back at the spiritual life again. But now it was too late. I couldn't climb on to the painted horse on the merry-go-round. The music had stopped. The figures were not going round and round anymore. And of course there was nobody to watch, nobody to enjoy it with, nobody to admire the way I had hopped from one painted animal to another. Is my misery because of some sin I committed in my youth and have never properly confessed? Or something to do with my glands? Should I try a psychiatrist? Should I consult a different priest? Am I a little mad? Should I drop all idea of the spiritual life, and stop wondering what God wants of me? Or on the other hand enter the religious life, and let them sort out what is the matter with me?"

The idea of a merry-go-round is not too far-fetched. The soul has been going around and around and getting nowhere. Its center has been itself instead of God who is responsible for the movement, the music, the mechanism, the whole thing. What the soul needs is to look for God and not find answers in self. Life is not a fairground anyway and the only way to live it is not to worry about what it is *like*, by one's own standards of judgment, but what it *is* by the quality of God's gift, and the gift is love. It is all in the Sermon on the Mount.

Perhaps it is only the greatest saints who really have no thought for themselves. It is not that contemplatives, more than any others, give themselves first place in their thoughts; it is that the interior life should not have the effect of making them want to dig down into their interiors. Their spirituality should make them rise above themselves, should make God the center of their thought, of their lives. It is partly the fault of the age in which we live that we examine our pasts, our motives, our reactions to good and evil. Even when we are not questioning the purposes of God, which our faith tells us we may not do, we are questioning our attitudes towards the purposes of God. This is surely one of the main blocks on the way to the heights, all the more of an obstacle because we imagine we are sorting ourselves out for the sake of serving God in greater purity. It is self-love disguised. Of most of our loves God is not jealous; it is of our self-love that God is jealous.

The third impediment to union is instability. The word "steadfastness" has an old-fashioned ring. But for progress in the interior life the will to continue, come what may, is an essential quality. Once again we are handicapped by our time. People change their jobs, their houses, their cars, their wives and husbands, if possible their physical appearances in a way probably not equalled in any other period of history. But it is not just the general tendency of the age which makes us restless in our relationship with God. It is much more the inability, until the final stage is reached, to find rest in God. Yet, as St. Augustine is so often quoted as saying, we can find rest in nothing short of God. So it is in the nature of the spiritual life, with its dark nights and its unsatisfied hungers, that inclines us to pick up and throw down, to try another dish and then leave it unfinished. Just as when suffering from flu we cannot lie still on the left side of the bed but must turn over to the right, only to find that the right is just as bad and perhaps the left will be easier after all, just as when carrying a heavy suitcase we shift from hand to hand, in the spiritual life we are constantly hoping to find what we are looking for in a new direction. A revelation dug up from the Middle Ages which promises peace to mankind? A recently discovered seer who prophesies imminent disaster? A message delivered by an angel to be broadcast in all languages on the radio? This is where the interior soul has to be careful, has need to remember the scriptural warnings about the devil's ability to come disguised as an angel of light, about false prophets seducing the credulous "and if possible even the elect," of signs and wonders which have no authority from God. This is where the interior soul has to meditate upon the jealousy of

God. Genuine manifestations have been granted in our time, proved by their fruits and leading only to the greater service of God, but it is the Church and not the press which must set its seal of authenticity. Frustrated souls, caught in the dark night and impatient to be out of it into the light of day, have been tricked into illuminism, spiritualism, and even ultimately diabolism. There can be few greater tragedies than to see deeply religious men and women, intended in the order of grace for the Unitive Way, being sidetracked by what might be called *over*-faith, but what in fact is superstition, into excesses which can only be playing into the hands of the devil. We grow impatient sometimes at the Church's slowness in recognizing Lourdes, Fatima, and other places blessed by Mary, but how fortunate we are to belong to a Church which knows what it is about in these matters.

The fourth obstacle to the prayer of mystical union is self-deception. This can be the most serious of them all because, of its nature, it is the most difficult to expose. We are not talking here of mistaken ideas which holy people can have about this or that religious issue; we are talking about courses of action, interior as well as exterior, deliberately held in opposition to grace on no more solid grounds than personal opinion. We have read of the failings of the saints, from St. Peter onward, but have we ever read of a saint who, with a clear mind, was guilty of self-deception?

Self-deception can go by the name of inconsistency, which is not as bad, and hypocrisy, which is worse, but essentially it is an offense against truth. We are all guilty of inconsistency, because it is almost impossible to steer between two principles which are both very nearly right. Each principle demands a decision which owes more to a third principle which is more important than either of them. Hypocrisy is easier to correct because the course taken is more clearly in conflict with the principle held. Not to correct it, or not to *try* to correct it, inevitably militates against advance in the spiritual life. Since the whole of the spiritual life is the all important quest for truth, inspired and crowned by truth, anything which deviates from truth is bound to be wrong. More or less, deliberately or in good faith, it is a contradiction.

Fortunately self-deception does not often carry us to great crises of faith and spirituality. Usually it operates over details, minor attitudes, prejudices, and emotional desires. Nevertheless it can be blinding, and souls suffering from it can excuse almost anything. Self-deception, even with the best will in the world, can come into nearly all we do, and the only remedy is to ask for more light with which to see how dishonest we are. Vainglory is a fruitful area for self-deception. We can spend hours before the Blessed Sacrament in prayer when it is only ostentation disguised. We can disguise the desire for recognition by calling it a desire to give help. Ambition we call desire for souls. Meanness in the matter of money we think of as holy poverty. In covering up our affections we can invent every kind of holy explanation. Blessed Henry Suso describes how two religious souls can justify their mutual attachment by claiming that the other is holier and that consequently each is deriving spiritual benefit from the relationship. "If the affection blinds," concludes Suso, "what difference does it make whether the speck in the eye is of gold dust or of coal dust?"

To the charge of worldliness the self-deceived man blandly replies "I don't know what you are talking about. I am only obeying St. Paul's remarks about being all things to all men: worldly with the worldly, spiritual with the spiritual." Another tactic of the self-deceived is to evade issues by substituting one temptation for another and justifying it on the grounds that one is guarding against committing sin. For example, a gambler drinks more than he should so as to avoid, so he tells himself, spending time and money at the tables. The drinker gambles so as to spend less time and money at the bar. It is like a man who has an earache in one ear hitting the other so hard that it will make him forget the pain in the first ear.

More immediately touching the prayer life is a particular self-deception about which St. John of the Cross goes on at great length. He is referring to supposedly divine locutions heard in the soul. "Great caution is necessary," he says, "so that we may not be deceived by these locutions. Let us not hold any of them in high esteem, but learn to direct our will to God with firm determination, fulfilling his law and his holy counsels perfectly, for this is the wisdom of the saints. Sometimes it is hardly possible to know what words are spoken by a good spirit and what by an evil spirit." He devotes no less than four chapters to this subject.[7] Lay people today might think that the question of locutions, true or false, was no longer a very common one. They would be surprised how often it comes up in retreats and in the confessional, and how difficult it is for a priest to make a judgment on it.

Passing over the greatest of all self-deceptions in the spiritual life, which is for a devout person to persuade himself that he is well into the Unitive Way when he is still far from it, we can now consider some of the characteristics which accompany, if not positively verify, that state. So far we have seen only some of those convoluted reasonings which keep people back from union and do no service to truth. We can now look at some of the more promising signs which, though they do not *prove* authenticity (because if they did there would be no more need for faith), at least indicate to the director, if not to the person himself, that the process is on the right lines.

In the Purgative Way the beginner's prayer was concerned with compunction and petition—the expression varied but the background showed chiefly contrition and request. In the Illuminative Way the prayer of the proficient, insofar as it could be pinned down at all, was acted out roughly to a theme song of trust and desire for relief. In the Unitive Way the dominant emotions would be love and gratitude.

"Since both my higher and my lower parts were at last at rest," says St. John of the Cross towards the end of the *Dark Night* where he is describing the state of union, "I went forth to the supernatural union of love with God . . . so the soul attains to peace and rest in a twofold manner, that is in its sensual and spiritual part." Later in the same penultimate chapter he goes even further: "This tranquility and peace of the spiritual house becomes an habitual and perfect property of the soul (insofar as this is possible according to the conditions of this life), by means of those substantial touches of divine union between the soul and the Son of God. . . . Divine Wisdom immediately unites itself with the soul by a new bond of loving possession."[8]

[7]*Ascent*, ch. 27-31.
[8]*Dark Night*, ch. 24.

St. Teresa says much the same thing when concluding her *Way of Perfection*. "You have now seen that it [the Lord's Prayer] comprises the whole spiritual road, right from the beginning until God absorbs the soul and gives it to drink abundantly of the fountain of living water which I told you was at the end of the road."[9]

Souls in the Unitive Way are sometimes surprised at how quickly the set times of prayer pass. Where before half an hour seemed long, now an hour seems short. Also in taking part in the Divine Office there is no longer the sense of a duty being performed, a culture to be studied, variant readings to be remembered; it is a conversation with personal associations and secrets which nobody else would understand, almost the kind of private language which children invent for communication with one another. If the sense of freedom described earlier suggested a happy-go-lucky indifference to the serious things of life, the impression must here be corrected. It is to be thought of more as the son's freedom of his Father's house—at-homeness, belonging.

In the last analysis the spiritual life's consummation is what our Lord said it would be. The seed is alive now because it has been prepared to die. The man has found his life, and is at home in it at last, because he was content to lose it. Even in this life he has received a hundredfold, in addition to what he can look forward to in the next, because by God's grace he has been granted to leave all and follow Christ.

"Lord," said Peter at the Transfiguration, "it is good for us to be here"(Mt. 17:4; Mk. 9:5; Lk. 9:33). If we were generous we should be able to repeat St. Peter's words wherever we are and at whatever stage of the spiritual life we happen to be in. Where we are is good because God has allowed it to be so, regardless of our feelings about it. If we are fanciful we can see in the three tabernacles which Peter wanted to build as a memorial of his experience the Purgative, the Illuminative, and the Unitive Ways. Or, and more fanciful still, the active, the contemplative, and the mixed life.

[9] *Way of Perfection*, ch. 42.